10-MINUTE OPTIONS TRADING AND ETF INVESTING

RAPIDLY BUILD WEALTH, RETIRE EARLY, AND LIVE
FREE FROM THE WORRY OF MARKET CRASHES

TRAVIS WILKERSON

HTTP://WWW.TRADERTRAVIS.COM

contained within this document, including, but not limited to— errors, omissions, or inaccuracies.

U.S. Government Required Disclaimer:

Options trading has large potential rewards and significant potential risks. You must be aware of the risks and be willing to accept them if you want to invest in the options markets. Don't trade with money you can't afford to lose. This book is neither a solicitation nor an offer to Buy/Sell options. No representation is being made that any account will or is likely to achieve profits or losses similar to those discussed in this book. The past performance of any trading system or methodology does not necessarily indicate future results. Before buying or selling an option, a person must receive a copy of "Characteristics and Risks of Standardized Options." Copies of this document may be obtained from your broker or any exchange on which options are traded.

CONTENTS

HOW TO GET THE MOST OUT OF THIS BOOK

Books are great, but sometimes you need additional resources to deepen your learning experience. Thus, I have put together a bonus package for readers of this book, where you will gain access to the following FREE resources:

- A seven-module option basics **video course.**
- A live case study of the **market-beating blueprint** taught in this book. You will see how I, a U.S. investing champion, make real-time decisions.
- You'll also gain access to my **trade journal Excel.** This way, you can see the history of my trades and what positions I'm currently in.

You will also get my emails with your case study. I share **my favorite option trading strategies**, ways to **protect your investments in any market**, and complimentary **alerts about trades I will place.** All these  bonuses are 100% free, with no strings attached. You only need to enter your email address. To get your bonuses, go to: www.tradertravis.com/bookbonus.html. Alternatively, scan the QR code.

PREFACE

 Every great dream begins with a dreamer.

— ATTRIBUTED TO HARRIET TUBMAN

What if you found a way to invest in the stock market where you got the gains of buy & hold <u>without</u> the account crushing losses?

- Would that ease some of your financial concerns and investment anxiety?
- Would that allow you to build wealth faster and possibly retire early?

Is it even possible to structure your investments in such a way? I did not think so until I was shown how to do it. I was blessed with this knowledge one day while sitting in church. It was March 13, 2011.

I should have been paying attention to the sermon but, as usual, I was, as my kids like to say, *'spacing out.'* While daydreaming, my mind was flooded with a flurry of insights regarding my investment portfolio. The ideas were coming so fast that I decided to grab a church notepad and write down the insights before I forgot them. When I got home, I tucked the paper in my idea folder and forgot about this market-beating strategy.

Figure 1 A snippet of the original notes before my tweaks

Now notice what I just said . . .

I was blessed with a plan and blueprint that showed me how to structure my investments to beat the market's performance and not lose a ton of money. However, I did nothing with the plan! You would think I would immediately jump on it and implement the strategy, but I did not.

I honestly cannot explain why I did not take action. The most likely reason is that I was busy with life's adult responsibilities, or maybe I did not explore the idea because subconsciously, I doubted it would work.

Like most, I had been programmed to believe that beating the stock market's performance over the long run was impossible. I had beaten the stock market's average performance before but did not have a twenty-year track record of doing it every year. However, I was not using the passive investing blueprint you will discover in this book. Instead, I was actively trading in the stock market, which has a high failure rate.

Two years would pass before I saw that piece of paper again. It was 2013, and I was proudly calculating my active trading return for the year, 30%. However, when my wife and I logged into our Vanguard retirement account, I noticed we earned 32% with a simple buy & hold strategy. We never even logged into that account, yet a passive approach beat my active trading approach. It was indeed a rude awakening for me.

Yes, I generated a respectable return of 30% on my money for the year. However, I had sorted through hundreds of stock charts during the year, spent countless hours at my computer, racked up thousands in broker commissions, and yet, the retirement account that we never even looked at did better.

For the first time in many years, I saw the flaw in active investing.

Around this time, I also read an article about the world's wealthiest individuals and noticed something I had never paid attention to before. **There were no active stock**

market traders on the list! The richest people in the world follow a passive approach to investing, not an active one. Thus, if I ever wanted to be ultra-wealthy, I knew a passive investment approach like buy & hold was the way to go.

However, there was only one problem. I do not like market crashes and hate losing 40–50% of my money in one go. Losing most of my 401(k) retirement account in the bear market of 2000–2002, with buy & hold, was one of the reasons I was attracted to active trading. I was disgusted with buy & hold and did not want to go down that road again. But that is when an internal voice reminded me of the blueprint I had long forgotten. It was a passive way to build wealth quickly while protecting you from market crashes.

However, I did not recognize those benefits at the time. To me, they were just notes and ideas scribbled on a piece of church paper. I was skeptical, but something about the plan felt right. I was drawn to it in an almost spiritual way. No matter how much I tried to dismiss the blueprint as impossible and unrealistic, the voice kept nudging me to try it.

And try, I did.

To my surprise, it worked brilliantly! However, I didn't tell anyone about my success, not even my wife. I thought I got lucky. The results seemed too good to be true. I was also scared that if I told other people about this method, it would stop working.

Eventually, I decided to tell one person, my wife.

Despite being a U.S. investing champion, first-generation millionaire, and someone who has not had a corporate job since he was 34, I STILL had self-doubt about sharing this publicly. However, my supportive wife encouraged me to share this market-beating blueprint with others.

Before I reveal it, let me set your expectations. I want to be crystal clear. All investing has risk, and I have not found a way to prevent losses entirely. However, I have found a way to reduce my risk of loss. Since using the blueprint taught in this book, I have beaten the market's long-term performance and avoided account-crushing losses. Because of this, I call it **enhanced buy & hold (or EBH for short)**. Once you see how it is structured, you will understand why it is named that.

So, if you are open-minded enough to explore the possibility of beating the market, I invite you on a journey. I will walk you down the same path I took a small group of students on. After testing it out personally for four or five years, I started teaching it to others. I had to make a few tweaks to accommodate how we are all wired differently emotionally.

Eventually, my clients duplicated my success in beating the market. Now it's your turn to try the enhanced buy & hold blueprint!

Here's to YOUR future success,

Trader Travis Wilkerson: The 10-Minute Investor™ & 2019 U.S. Investing Champion (options division)

INTRODUCTION

You can be free. You can live and work anywhere in the world. You can be independent from routine and not answer to anybody. This is the life of a successful trader.

— ALEXANDER ELDER

In my first book, *Options Trading Made Simple (OTMS)*, I taught options trading basics and profiled an active trading strategy. The book was written for beginner options traders who prefer to time the stock market and get in or out based on the market's overall trend. I also shared the blueprint I used to achieve financial freedom in five years.

In *OTMS*, I also introduced a simple passive trading strategy. It is called the Buffett call option, and I modeled it after Warren Buffett's long-term options approach. The Buffett call is a part of the enhanced buy & hold blueprint. Thus, it will be profiled more in this book. And that leads to who this book is for and who not.

Who this book is not for . . .

This is not a reference book or a book for people looking for general knowledge. It is more of a blueprint, and it's for option traders and buy & hold investors who already have some experience with investing and want a simple proven system to follow. This book speaks to those who prefer a more passive approach to investing. More specifically, people who want:

1. High investment returns.
2. Protection against market crashes. And . . .
3. Only to spend roughly 10 minutes a year managing their portfolio.

Essentially, this book is for those who want to make money and also have a life in the process. Those who want the profits of stock market trading without the endeavor turning into another full-time job. That means there will not be any talk of Beta, Alpha, Black-Scholes, Bollinger bands, RSI, Day trading, Deep-in-the-money, Delta, Vega, Gamma, Rho, Theta, Double tops, Support and Resistance, Volatility, Intrinsic and Extrinsic Value, or the VIX (gasp). Many of those are sacred, and options traders think they must master them to succeed, but they are incorrect.

My experience and investment results prove that you don't need all those tools. To date, I haven't found a person who uses all of the above that can beat my investment returns over a three- to five-year period of time. Why? Because my 10-minute trading system is simple, and in my experience, a simple system beats a complicated one any day of the week.

Also, this book only focuses on 'buying options.' Many misinformed people in the options community believe buying options is risky and you will lose money overall. They are wrong! And in this book, you'll discover a prudent and successful way of buying options. That means we won't go into depth on how to 'sell options' or any of the strategies that apply to that. That hence also implies no thorough lessons on credit spreads, covered calls, cash-secured puts, butterfly spreads, calendar spreads, etc. Instead, I will profile a simple option buying blueprint that is paired up with an exchange-traded fund (or ETF for short).

Now let me speak to buy & hold investors . . .

We will not discuss how to pick individual stocks; doing it successfully takes more time and work than most people realize. We also won't focus on IPOs, sector rotation, chasing stock splits, or looking for the next 'hidden gem poised to increase 1,000 fold in the next few years.' I'm not saying the above doesn't work, but you don't need to know any of that to succeed with the blueprint taught in this book. Right now, you may be thinking, *"Geez, Travis. You gave me a list of everything you won't cover. Are you trying to make me not want to read your book?"* No, I just want to ensure this book is precisely what you want.

So, who is this book for?

It's for people who want to be shown precisely how a U.S. investing champion manages his money. It's for busy people who don't have the time to sort through hundreds of stock charts daily, looking for trades or investments. Again, it's for people who want high investment returns, protection against market crashes, and only want to spend a few minutes a year managing their portfolio. People who want to make money quickly, make it safely, and avoid going broke in the process.

And the best way I've discovered how to do that is through enhanced buy & hold (or EBH for short). **EBH is traditional buy & hold, paired up with buying stock options**.

- You buy put options for peace of mind and market crash protection.
- You then buy call options for accelerated growth.
- Lastly, you buy shares of a broad-based S&P 500 index fund/ETF for safe and stable returns.

The enhanced portion of the blueprint comes from the option trades. Sadly though, only a few people have heard about options. The few who have heard about options are usually told to stay away from them. That's despite trillions of dollars flowing through the options market each year (Detrixhe, 2021). Even *Forbes*, a magazine that caters to the wealthy, educates their readership on using stock options (Light, 2022).

This is a perfect example of why the rich get richer and the poor get poorer. Rich people are educated on options and encouraged to use them, while ordinary people like you and I are told to avoid them. As one millionaire told me, *"If you want to get rich, do as rich people do."* And rich people are using options in their overall investment plan. The good news is that you will discover how they use options to build and protect their wealth in this book.

Now let's talk about buy & hold, the granddaddy of all passive stock market investing. It's more widely known, and many are encouraged to make it their default method of investing. Here in America, it's the engine that powers the large majority of retirement accounts for our working citizens. It has also made many people wealthy beyond their wildest dreams. However, it has a few downfalls. It's a painfully slow process, and you have little control over how much money you make and how much you lose during market crashes.

And that's where options trading comes into the picture. I combine buy & hold with stock options. The combo allows me to earn outsized returns in up markets and protects me against losing money during market crashes. Best of all, the entire portfolio can be set up in just a few minutes.

- It can be implemented at any time and in any market environment.
- There is no market timing involved. I don't have to look at a stock chart or technical indicator to place the trades.
- Best of all, I only focus on one stock/ETF and generate returns of 12%, 32%, or even 45% on my money each year. Of course, your results will vary.

And if those statements sound too good to be true, trust me, I get it. That's why I'm not asking for your complete trust and faith. If you are of the mindset that you'll believe it when you see it, then great! That's *precisely* the kind of attitude I want you to have. I don't want you to accept these concepts until you see them work in your own life.

Trust is earned. I only ask that you temporarily suspend any disbelief long enough to try these concepts out yourself. I want you to do what the United States Military taught me, *'trust, but verify.'* Also, as an author, I want to do my best to support you, so here are three easy ways you can verify my claims. I perform the first two.

<u>Verification method #1</u>: Read the case study chapter of this book. You will see a real-world example of how the enhanced buy & hold concepts worked from 2010–2023. These will be the actual results of the EBH blueprint's performance, using the stock and option pricing from the above dates. And since past performance does not guarantee that future performance will be the same, I am providing method #2.

<u>Verification method #2</u>: Download the book bonuses and watch me invest my real money using the strategy taught within these pages. You'll discover that the techniques work as advertised in the book, but you won't have to believe me. You'll see it with your own eyes. **Enhanced buy & hold is a simple combination of trades I place once a year, and it takes me less than 10 minutes to set up.** It's how I got the nickname *"The 10-Minute Investor ™."*

Even this verification method is not enough because all success is autobiographical! Just because the concepts taught in this book work for me doesn't mean they will work for you. Even though I've been able to teach other people how to beat the stock market successfully, it does not mean you will have success. Because of that, we have the last and most crucial verification method.

<u>Verification method #3</u>: As I tell all of my coaching clients, *"Watching my trades won't put money into your pocket. You eventually have to do the work."* However, it's scary at first; I get that. That's why I suggest you take a low-risk

approach to testing these concepts yourself. It's called paper or virtual trading. Paper or virtual trading is where you go through all the motions of investing, but you don't use real money. You simulate investing, but you use fake or paper money.

One of the many reasons for paper trade is that it's a cautious approach that ensures you learn how to implement the strategies correctly. I don't think you should invest real money until you understand what you are doing. Thus, paper trading for at least six months would be prudent. You don't want to lose money unnecessarily. When you're new to investing or trading options, it takes a while to master the technical aspects of it. But once you learn the mechanics, you can slowly transition to real money, where you discover how to manage the emotional part of investing.

In conclusion, there are numerous ways to invest and different topics we can cover regarding ETFs and options trading. However, I'm only an expert in what I use to earn additional income, protect my investments, and experience freedom in my life. Thus, this book only focuses on one method of investing, the one I used to rapidly build wealth, retire early, and live free from the worry of market crashes.

Within these pages, I'm sharing the <u>proven investment</u> <u>blueprint</u> I used to become a first-generation millionaire and a U.S. investing champion. I hope these concepts can bless your life as much as mine. I even provide three ways to verify that this is a legit strategy. However, no matter how hard I try, there will always be a group of investors who will not verify the claims made in this book.

As a cautionary tale, I'll share details about their behaviors in the next chapter. Please ensure you don't end up in one of these two groups because if you do, you will fail with the enhanced buy & hold blueprint. Having the right mindset with what I share in this book is essential. You will not get the same results as me if you have a conflicting belief system. That said, I'll see you in the next chapter.

1

ARE YOU A BIGOT OR INTELLECTUAL SNOB?

 Never be limited by other people's limited imaginations.

— MAE JEMISON

Since using the enhanced buy & hold blueprint, I've beaten the market's long-term performance and avoided account-crushing losses. However, I think it would be silly for you to *automatically believe me* just because I said that's what I've accomplished. That would be naïve.

I know that some trust has to be earned, so in the introduction, I asked you to temporarily suspend any disbelief long enough for you to try this out yourself. Said another way, I want you to be an action taker. I'll provide all the rules and a step-by-step template, but you must see if this blueprint works for you.

However, that's what I want. You ultimately have to decide for yourself. And you know what? Some don't decide. They instead choose to be intellectual snobs (also called critics). They stand on the sidelines, poke holes in everything, and tell you all the 'theoretical' reasons why something won't work. They are always too lazy to roll up their sleeves and put in the work to *verify* the claims of someone.

Maybe critics fear failure or have been let down so often that they're bitter. Who knows? All I know is that they are out there, and their onslaught of negativity almost discouraged me from sharing this information with you. I'm glad I ultimately decided to ignore them.

That said, here is my stern warning to intellectual snobs (aka critics). This book is not for you if you don't believe you can beat the stock market over time. It will challenge the dogma you hold to be true, and you'll fail with the blueprint because reality is manifested out of your beliefs. Now, let's move on to the next group of people who will fail with these concepts, bigots . . .

BUY & HOLD BIGOTS

I'm excited to share my market-beating blueprint with you, but I initially hesitated to write this book out of fear that my message would be rejected. I first tried to share what I had discovered with a group of buy & hold investors I admired. It was a massive failure. They rejected me and my message, and I became discouraged. Over time, I got over my feelings and decided this message was too important to keep to myself.

So, what is my message?

It's simple; I believe you can consistently beat the stock market average. However, because of this message, I am always in direct conflict with a group of people I call buy & hold bigots. They are fanatics who tell me it is impossible to beat the stock market average over the long haul. Yet, somehow, my enhanced buy & hold portfolio has done it consistently while taking on less risk.

Pause . . .

What thoughts or emotional reactions did you have to me saying I beat the market? Did you automatically reject the possibility of truth in that simple statement? *"Yeah, right . . . no way . . . sounds too good to be true."* Only naïve people would accept such a statement on absolute faith without evidence. However, a wise person, free of sickening self-limitation, would merely ask, *"How do you beat the market,*

Travis? Tell me more." If that's your response, this book is for you, but first . . .

I must acknowledge the guy who inspired me to share my investing blueprint with the world. His name is Chris M., and I met him at a financial blogger conference. Chris is loosely part of a small but growing movement called F.I.R.E., which stands for Financial Independence, Retire Early. I associate with the movement, but I'm not welcome in their club, even though I achieved financial freedom when I was 34. Maybe I am welcome, and I'm just being a highly sensitive diva. Yeah, that's most likely it . . . and my wife agrees. So let me rephrase that. I *'feel'* unwelcome because most are buy & hold bigots.

Bigots are people who are intolerant toward those holding different opinions. They tend to chastise anyone who doesn't believe what they believe. These buy & hold bigots also have nothing good to say about actively trading the stock market. They usually, not always, but typically stereotype active investors like me and are closed-minded to what I have to teach. They say things like . . .

- *"You can't time the market."*
- *"Dollar cost averaging into a broad-based index fund is the way to go."*
- *"Active trading is a loser's game, and you can't consistently beat the stock market average over a long period of time."*

- *"It's impossible to beat the professionals at their own game as you don't have their knowledge, training, or resources."*
- **"Options trading is risky. You say you trade options like Warren Buffett, but he hates options. Quoting Buffett might draw readers, but your methods obviously have nothing to do with the investing legend."**

All the above bullet points are firmly held beliefs that are stated as facts. In life, you can find many examples that prove these statements false. The last bullet point exemplifies the dangers of being a bigot. You look stupid when you speak with authority, but you are wrong.

Bigotry = Ignorance!

I trade options, and the most profitable strategy I have ever discovered, I learned from Warren Buffett. That's right, the *"investing legend"* uses options via his company Berkshire Hathaway Inc. (Cfa, 2009). It's hard for anyone to convince me that Buffett hates options when he has used them to earn billions in profit. So if you're a buy & hold bigot who thinks Mr. Buffett hates options, take the time to read his shareholder letters where he outlines the options strategy he occasionally uses.

Moving on . . .

Buy & hold fanatics proudly brag about their *'average returns'* while vilifying active investors like me. When the stock market crashes, and 40–50% of their money evaporates, they rally together and say, *"This is normal. The market runs in cycles. Just keep investing."* My translation: bend over and take the loss because this is normal. If getting screwed financially and watching my account massively drop in value is normal, then, no thanks; I want a new normal!

I'm not the only one. Most students come my way because they are fed up with that investing style. Watching 50% of your money disappear while you helplessly sit there and watch it happen is terrifying. It's even worse for retirees. A loss like that often causes them to reenter the corporate world when they should be traveling the world and enjoying retirement.

Buy & hold is fantastic until you experience the flaws firsthand. So I understand why people want to learn how to trade the stock market actively. I get it! However, before we move on to active trading, a quick investing example to defend buy & hold.

Please note: I will use figures from my broker's historical pricing feature or actual transactions I placed in my account for any examples I provide in the book. If using historical data, I use the prices listed at the end of the trading day. Also, I round the figures to the nearest dollar in many examples. That said, let's cover an example of buy & hold.

Figure 2 Stock chart of SPY, Source: StockCharts.com

The start date is January 14, 2021. You buy 400 shares of SPDR S&P 500 ETF Trust (stock symbol: SPY, often pronounced as S.P.Y. or simply spy). It's an exchange-traded fund (ETF) that tracks the S&P 500. ETFs will be explained in a later chapter, but for now, know the price of the ETF at the time of purchase was $378.46. So the total investment was $151,384 for 400 shares. Fast forward to January 18, 2022, and SPY has risen in price to $456.49.

That's a gain of $31,212, or 20.6%, on your 400 shares. That's outstanding! And what did you have to do to earn that profit? Absolutely nothing! The beauty of buy & hold is that you benefit from the long-term trend of American capitalism. You put your money into the stock market, sit back, and earn passive income with little to no effort.

Now let's move forward another year to January 19, 2023. SPY is trading at $388.64 a share. **You lost $27,140, or -14.9%.** You have lost most of last year's profit and are essentially back to where you started in 2021. Two years of your life have passed, and you've made a small profit overall.

Figure 3 Stock chart of SPY during the 2022 Bear Market, Source: StockCharts.com

The previous profit and loss example illustrates how investing can sometimes be an emotional and financial roller coaster. Remember that this type of movement is typical, and it's the price we pay to get rich in the stock market. Also, passive income in the stock market works both ways. If you make money passively, you can also lose it passively. Making money with little to no effort on your part is fun. However, losing it from being passive makes you feel completely helpless.

Before we move on, let me be crystal clear. Yes, buy & hold works. There is an overwhelming amount of evidence proving that buy & hold works. I don't dispute that. However, what angers me is that financial experts push it down people's throats without empathy for the financial and emotional destruction it causes when things go wrong. Especially for retirees who count on that money lasting for the rest of their lives.

Watching 40–50% of my money disappear and then doing nothing about it is reckless. That's why I dislike traditional buy & hold. It does not adequately protect you during market crashes. So, if that's the problem, what is my proposed solution?

I'll get to my current solution in a later chapter, but the first solution I tried was actively trading the stock market. With active trading, you control your gains and losses more. And as you'll see in an upcoming example, you can often make as much, or more money, than buy & hold while risking less money. Sadly though, the benefits of actively managing your money can also make you a bigot.

WHY I USED TO BE AN ACTIVE TRADING BIGOT

Bigotry is also present in the active trading community. I know because I used to be one. I thought buy & hold investors were stupid to settle for 7–9% a year when I was earning 15–30% by actively trading the stock market. I was biased because of my real-world experience with active trading.

Let me show an example of why I was such a bigot, and I will explain the mechanics of the investment that produced this type of return in a later chapter. We will use the same start and end dates as earlier, January 14, 2021 to January 18, 2022. However, I will buy six call option contracts instead of stock shares. Again, I'll explain the mechanics of options in a later chapter, but for now, follow the big picture. Options are an investment tool that allows you to benefit from stock price movement without owning the stock. Moving on . . .

I'll start with the same $151,384 I have to invest, but this time, I'll only use roughly 20% of it to buy call options. On January 14, 2021, I purchased six December 2023, 380 call options @ $4,877 per contract, a total investment of $29,262. Fast forward to January 18, 2022, and I was able to sell those calls for $10,429 per contract (a $5,552 profit per contract). Since I bought six contracts, that's a total gain of $33,312 or 113.8%.

Now let's compare the two approaches . . .

- With buy & hold, I invested $151,384 to make a profit of $31,212 or 20.6% on my original investment. Note: 100% of my money was at risk of loss to get that return.

- With call options, I invested $29,262. Less than 1/5 of the buy & hold investment. Yet, I walked away with a profit of $33,312, or a 113.8% return on my original investment. I didn't invest all my money, but that $33K profit grew my overall account by 22%.

With options, I had a bigger profit, a higher percent return, and I risked less of my money! I grew my overall account by 22% while leaving most of it safely in cash, protected from a market crash. Can you see how fifteen-plus years of performance like that would make me biased? As you can see, I can often beat the market's average return with active trading.

Right now, some critic of options is ready to send me hate mail about how this example is misleading and doesn't talk about losses. If so, chill out, crabby pants! I'll get to the risk of losing money with options next. I'm merely showing how my experience with options made me an active trading bigot.

That said, let's talk about losing money. Yes, the call option return of 113.8% was incredible, but don't get so excited that you forget the outsized return also works in reverse. It's best never to forget that. How would you feel if you had lost 100% of your investment? Because that is what almost happened the year after this significant gain. If you buy a new set of call options and fast forward another year to January 19, 2023, the next round of calls loses $26,700. This is similar to the buy & hold loss of $27,140 during the same period. However, the 67.9% percent loss on the options is stomach-churning.

Too many investors are so enticed by the big profits that options deliver that they get sloppy, risk too much money, and eventually lose it all. I've seen it happen too many times in my twenty-plus-year career. Heck, it happened to me a few times early in my journey. It almost happened to me again in the bear market of 2022, but I was smart enough to correct my errors before they caused too much financial damage. This illustrates that sometimes I make mistakes, or often life gets in the way of active trading, and I fail to beat the performance of a simple buy & hold approach.

In summary, both approaches have pros and cons. In my experience, integrating the best of both worlds is the best solution. And that is precisely what we will discuss in the next chapter.

2

WHEN INVESTING ENEMIES JOIN TOGETHER, MORE MONEY CAN BE MADE

In the financial meltdown of 2008, my accounts were devastated, and I became so exasperated that I called my fund managers. These "professional" investors told me, 'Well, everyone had losses, we all lost money . . . it'll come back.' What really bothered me was the fact that they still charged me tens of thousands of dollars in fees — TO LOSE MY MONEY!

I was extremely frustrated, to say the least, and decided at that moment I had to take control of my money [and learned how to trade options]. I now have the skill to rebuild my retirement account and create a weekly earning FOR LIFE. Needless to say, I have fired all of my "professional funds managers!" In a very short period of time, I have taken what was left of my retirement account and increased it by 163%.

— MICHELLE F.

I started an online coaching program in 2010 to teach investors how to be active option traders. I received the above note from one of the graduates of that class. Michelle, like I, was fed up with the flaws and dangers of buy & hold. The pain of a massive buy & hold loss is also why I became an active trader.

However, is active trading better than buy & hold? I used to think so, but as I got older, I discovered it's not sustainable long term. Do you remember in the Preface where I shared how our buy & hold retirement account beat my active trading account in 2013?

Yes, I generated a respectable return of 30% on my money for the year. However, I had sorted through hundreds of stock charts during the year, spent countless hours at my computer, racked up thousands in broker commissions, and yet, our retirement account, which we never even looked at, did better.

I saw the flaw in active investing for the first time in years. As an active trader, I was used to earning 15–30% yearly returns. I won the U.S. Investing Championship with a return of 31.6% in one year. However, with active stock market trading, you need the following:

- Lots of free time and a stoic-like personality.
- A calm demeanor where you keep irrational emotions under control.
- Little to no stress in your personal life.
- And you also need the mental capacity to handle the demands of active investing.

Thus, you will struggle with active stock market trading if you have a busy work life or many personal demands on your time. It's precisely why active investing has such a high failure rate.

Think about it. What's the demographic of most active or day trading gurus online? Most of them are young with no kids . . . people who traditionally have much more free time than a parent or middle-aged corporate worker. Conversely, do many sixty-year-old day trading gurus promote their courses online?

There are *old traders* and *active traders,* but there aren't many old active traders. There's a reason for that. The older group has discovered something, but the younger ones have not—something I learned in 2013 when I was busy building a coaching business and was mentally burnt out. It showed in my trading performance.

The lesson: Your active trading performance will suffer when you suffer. Your results depend highly on you and what you have going on in your personal life. If you bring your A-game to active trading, you can often beat the market's average return. However, when you perform less than your best, you underperform.

Thus, passive investing is the best approach for busy people. Despite its apparent flaws, my eyes were finally opened to the fact that **buy & hold 'is' one of the most passive ways to build wealth**. The benefit of passive investing is that it still sets you up for success, but your results aren't heavily dependent on your moves. You simply invest your money in the stock market and let the market do all the hard work for you.

Passive investing is like starting a business and hiring employees to do all the work. Active investing is like starting a business where you do all the work yourself. You handle accounting, marketing, sales, product fulfillment, customer support, etc. It's exhausting!

- So, how about your life? Is it perfect?
- Do you have an abundance of free time?
- Does everything always go as planned?

That's a big fat no in my life, so I switched to passive investing. However, I refuse to completely abandon options because they give me more control over my income, and I make too much money with them. The best solution I have found is to integrate the best of both worlds. And that is what we will discuss next.

BUY & HOLD + OPTIONS TRADING

After my active trading disappointment, I needed to shift how I invested my money. However, it was difficult to change my investing style after using it for 15+ years. It took a mindset shift I frankly wasn't ready for. I assume it had the same effect on me as someone who has worked for a company for 15 years and then gets laid off. You're a bit lost initially and must find your way again. You're essentially starting all over again.

Regardless, I needed a strategy to accommodate the changes in my personal life. When I started as an active trader, I was young, single, and had no kids. Then I got married, had three kids, and got older. And with age and more responsibilities came a harder season of life.

I held on to active trading as long as I could, but I eventually had to say goodbye. Again, shifting from active options trading to enhanced buy & hold investing took work. It is best to be open-minded for enhanced buy & hold to work well.

Remember, I was an active trading bigot at the time. It was also challenging because I had to learn from buy & hold bigots who tried to program me with their limiting beliefs. For example, many disagreed with my views on beating the market and immediately dismissed the idea. Again, that's the exact kind of bigoted mindset I cautioned you about in a previous chapter.

Bigots will fail with enhanced buy & hold and won't beat my investment returns because they are too stubborn to see the simple truths right before their faces. <u>Please note</u>: I'm speaking about myself. My bigotry closed my eyes to other 'truths' that could benefit my life.

Luckily, I met a millionaire who taught me a better way of thinking. He said, *"Don't be an 'either or thinker.' Be a 'both' thinker. Don't think buy & hold versus active options investing. Think both. Learn both methods, implement the best of each approach, and get double the benefit."*

It makes perfect sense when you stop and think about it, but again, bigotry closes your eyes to other ways of seeing the world. This is highly evident in the world of politics. I've noticed that people who are dogmatic and inflexible in their thinking tend to make horrible investors over the long term. Again, this is my opinion; it doesn't make it a fact.

Regardless, my current stance on bigotry is that I let the dummies debate the details!

The war between buy & hold investors and active traders is exhausting—a battle I was once a part of. Now I let those idiots get into pointless arguments about the best method. While those dummies debate details, curious and open minds study both approaches. And that leads to the secret to 'how' I can consistently beat the stock market average.

I integrate buy & hold with options trading! I combined 'conservative' buy & hold with 'conservative' options trading to earn 12%, 32%, or even 45% on my money each year. Of course, your results may vary.

To illustrate this point, let's first review and then combine the two approaches covered in the previous chapter. Here they are again for your reference:

- With buy & hold, we invested $151,384 to make a profit of $31,212, or a 20.6% return on the original investment. Note: 100% of the money was at risk of loss to get that return.
- With call options, we invested $29,262. Yet, we walked away with a profit of $33,312, or a 113.8% return on the original investment. Note: Roughly 80% of the account was in cash, uninvested, and protected from market crashes.

Now let's combine the approaches to make up <u>two of the three parts</u> of the enhanced buy & hold portfolio. We will start with the total buy & hold investment of $151,384, but we will strategically split the money between stock shares and option contracts.

- $29,262 will be devoted to six call option contracts.
- The remaining $122,122 will go towards buying 322 shares of SPY.

In this example, most of the money is devoted to buy & hold as the long-term risk of losing money is lower, and the rest is dedicated to the riskier option trades. It's roughly an 80/20 split. It is just enough money in options to give you a nice profit boost in up markets, but not so much that you get destroyed financially when the market falls in price. As I stated in my book *Options Trading Made Simple*, **the way to win with options is to risk less money, not more.**

Okay, let me return to the example before I lose my train of thought . . .

We have invested the same $151K as we did with pure buy & hold, and we are using the exact start and end dates, January 2021 to January 2022. Now let's see the results of this 80/20 setup:

- A $25,126 profit on the 322 stock shares, or a 20.6% return on investment.
- And a $33,312 profit on the six call options, or a 113.8% return on investment.

The combined profit of $58,438 allowed us to grow our overall account by 38.6% in one year, while the pure buy & hold return was only 20.6%. This enhanced performance is what I discovered once I stopped being a bigot. **By combing the best of both approaches, I make more money!**

However, don't salivate over that incredible return because the returns will be slightly lower when you see the complete enhanced buy & hold portfolio. Regardless, when people tell me that options are risky and I can't beat the return of buy & hold, I smile and silently say to myself, *"You can keep your opinion, and I'll keep all the money I'm making from doing what you say is impossible."*

Now that I have tickled your greed gland, let's pause here to talk about losing money (again). I want to caution you about following this buy & hold + call blueprint long term. It has two potential downfalls. The first is that the high returns will trigger your emotions, but not in a good way. Making money quickly is intoxicating and causes people to be too greedy over time.

The second downfall is that the losses can be so significant in down markets that it triggers panic emotions. Adding calls to your buy & hold portfolio will give you super performance, but the tradeoff is that it puts you in a position to lose more than the market when prices fall. Here is an example of the panic emails I get from people who didn't listen to my warnings about risking too much money on calls:

"I lost 80% of the value of my calls. My account is down more than the market. I'm losing too much money! What can I do?"

That statement is EXACTLY why you shouldn't focus on the fast growth of calls. With investing, you want to avoid anything that will trigger your emotions. When emotions are high, intelligence is down. Want proof? Think about controversial presidential elections. Don't ordinary intelligent people lose their minds and act like idiots? Why? Because their emotions are triggered. Enough politics; let me ask you an important question . . .

What puts people <u>out of business</u>, making lots of money, or losing lots of money?

It's not a trick question, I promise. I'm asking because people rarely think about it. When people see the results of the buy & hold + call blueprint, I'd estimate 97% of them focus on how much money it made. Oddly enough, trying to make a tremendous amount of money is not how I, or many others, achieved financial freedom. I didn't get rich when I focused solely on making money. Instead, I kept failing.

However, when I focused on avoiding the activities that cause people to go broke or lose too much money, that's when building wealth became easier. So, when you encounter an opportunity that has the potential to increase your wealth rapidly, you have to stop and force yourself to focus on where things can go wrong. Then you make a plan to avoid financial ruin. After that's done, then and only then do you focus on the money-making opportunity.

That said, in a few chapters, I'll share my solution to avoiding financial ruin. It was an adjustment I made to the blueprint. After walking others through this blueprint, I noticed some, like me, were not bothered by losses, while others became emotionally unraveled.

Thus, I made a few tweaks to accommodate that we are all emotionally wired differently. I added a market crash component, so people didn't freak out from losing money so quickly in down markets. I also made the options portion of the blueprint more passive to align with the passive nature of buy & hold. And that last tweak helped clients develop more discipline and patience—two of the necessary ingredients for financial success.

Now let's wrap up this chapter with a criticism I received about my high performance.

By combining the best of both approaches, I've earned above-average market returns, even though my total financial investment was similar to traditional buy & hold. Of course, I'm not implying you can do that or will. I'm just sharing what I've been able to do. Similar to the time I tried to share with a group of buy & hold investors what I had accomplished with options trading. It was on the blog of a famous finance guru who goes by the name of Mr. Money Mustache. However, in the comment section, here is what one buy & hold critic had to say about my options trading return in 2015:

> "*Just so people know. Options Trading CAN be very profitable via dumb luck, especially when you're at the volatile end of a bull market. You can get lucky and exploit people who think the market will continue to rise like it did in 2012 thru 2014. You can also get very lucky trading on the volatility. I'm not surprised that someone made a 211% return in the options market last year. I just question anyone who advertises it as anything but dumb luck. One data point achieved during a perfect storm of economic events does not make for sound long-term investing advice*"
>
> — (WHAT TO DO ABOUT THIS SCARY STOCK MARKET, 2016)

Sigh . . . First, let's get a few things straight here. I can't make any promises about what you can or will achieve. But I do promise to show you what has worked for me and the exact steps I've taken to earn additional income, protect my investments, and experience freedom in my life. That's my new mission now that I'm free from the rat race of corporate America. I'm now teaching regular people how to invest safely, confidently, and profitably.

Second, in my previous example, you saw how the calls generated a 113.8% return on our investment. Those results are easily verifiable. Thus, it shouldn't be too much of a stretch to consider that one could earn 211% with options. Then again, critics never take the time to verify.

Third, I take full responsibility for the events that led to my message being rejected. In my excitement to share what I had achieved, I didn't stop to think if that was the right audience for the message. It clearly wasn't. So let me be a little blunter to ensure the message I preach is for you.

If you are a closed-minded buy & hold bigot, please go elsewhere. You honestly aren't qualified to learn my strategies. It will severely challenge your worldview. What I teach is not for ignorant people or people who want to be average. It's only for people who desire to be 'above average' . . . people who are 'open-minded' . . . and people who want to be in a position to have 'dumb luck' like me. If that's you, continue on.

The following chapters will introduce you to the three enhanced buy & hold components: call options, put options, and index fund investing. You'll also discover the precise rules I follow.

3

HOW TO RAPIDLY BUILD WEALTH

*Over a seven year period, I can tell you unequivo-
cally wealth is not a function of gender, not a function of race. It is not a function of circumstance. It
is not a function of condition—how the cards were
dealt, which side of the town you were born on, but
it is a function of choice, a function of discipline,
and it is a function of effort, faith, and believing in
yourself.*

— DR. DENNIS KIMBRO

In the previous chapter, I shared how a buy & hold
fanatic implied that my 211% return on my money in
2015 resulted from *"dumb luck."* In this chapter, I will
describe the tool that allowed me to have such dumb luck.
It was call options (or calls for short). It's also the tool that

allowed me to **rapidly build wealth** and achieve financial freedom in a short period of time.

To set your expectations, I will not be detailing my moves to earn that 211%. I'm looking at those trades right now in my trade journal Excel. However, they are from my active trading days, and I no longer invest that way. Again, active trading is, in my experience, not sustainable long term. With a few family deaths, caring for an aging parent, a divorce, or if life generally gets in the way, you will struggle with active options trading.

I'm now a passive options trader and only trade roughly once a year. The tradeoff is that my performance is slightly lower. However, I can live with that tradeoff because I now have more free time. And at my age, having more time is more valuable than a few more dollars in my bank account. Personal freedom is priceless!

CALL OPTION BASICS

In *Options Trading Made Simple*, the first book in this series, I thoroughly covered stock options basics. Since this is the second book in the series, and for the sake of brevity, I won't rehash all of that material here. I will, however, touch on the big-picture overview of call options so you can understand why they are a vital component of the enhanced buy & hold portfolio. Afterward, if you need more knowledge, please read

Options Trading Made Simple, or review free options basics tutorials online.

Call options don't represent ownership like stock shares but are contracts that grant you specific rights. They are similar to real estate contracts. With a real estate purchase contract:

- You have the <u>right to purchase</u> a 'property' at a <u>set price</u> on or before a <u>specific date</u>. The contract expires after this date.
- You also have to put down a small deposit or <u>premium</u>.

And when you 'buy' a call option contract:

- You have the <u>right to purchase</u> 'stock' at a <u>set price</u> on or before a <u>specific date</u>. The contract expires after this date.
- You also have to put down a small deposit or <u>premium</u>.
- Also, options are contracts between two parties. So if you exercised the above rights, the seller of the call would be obligated to sell you the shares you wanted to buy.

See, options aren't that hard to understand, are they? That said, let's go into a little more detail. Options are relatively unknown to most stock market investors. And those who have heard about options are often told they are risky and should be avoided. This statement is primarily made out of ignorance because stock options were created to protect investors from risk (Contributor, 2019). In the case of call options, they were created so investors could place small bets on a stock's price movement without tying up large sums of money.

- A person who **buys one call option** has the right, but not the obligation, to buy 100 stock shares at a set price on or before a specific date.
- When the rights of the option contract are exercised, the price the stock can be bought at is the **option's strike price.**
- Since you are only buying a contract and not 100 shares of the stock, you only have to pay a small fee, known as the **premium**. Option premiums, or prices, are always listed as small numbers, but since the option contract controls 100 shares of stock, you have to multiply the premium by 100 to get the trust cost of buying the option.
- The contract also has an **expiration date** and is only valid for a certain period of time.
- Because of the limited shelf life, the options suffer from a concept called **time decay.**

A little more about time decay before we move on. Part of an options premium, or cost, is time value. It's a dollar figure assigned to how many days are left until the option expires. For example, options with longer expirations cost more because they provide more 'time' to be right about your options bet.

Over time, the option's price dwindles in value due to a concept called time decay. Time decay describes how the value of an options contract decreases as the option approaches its expiration date. A small portion of the option's value is lost each day that passes. It starts as a slow decline and then speeds up the closer the option gets to its expiration date because there is less time to realize a profit from the trade. Picture an ice cube. You take it out of the freezer and put it in the sun. It starts melting slowly, but the longer it's in the sun, the faster it will melt.

Now, let's look at an example call option trade: I buy one SPY December 15, 2023, 380 call option @ $48.77:

- This one call option gives me the right, but not the obligation, to buy one hundred shares of SPY.
- 380 is the strike price or the price for which I can purchase the stock.
- $48.77 is the option's premium (the actual cost is $4,877).
- And the contract is only valid up until its expiration date of December 15, 2023. I have until

this date to exercise the rights of the contract (i.e., buy the stock).

Here's a hypothetical example of how calls can be used. Let's say an investor wanted to buy 100 shares of stock XYZ @ $160 a share price. It would cost $16,000. If the stock went up in price, they would make money. However, if the stock falls in price, they could lose all $16,000. If the investor is nervous or unsure, they could buy a three-year 160 strike call option on stock XYZ for $10 (or $1,000) instead.

So, for three years, the investor could monitor the stock. Because of the rights of the call contract, it will increase in value as the stock rises in price (and vice versa). This is also why options are known as derivatives. Their cost is derived from the price of something else, such as a stock or ETF.

- Suppose the investor gets lucky, and the stock increases to $190. They could exercise the rights of the call contract and buy the stock for $160 (a $30 discount).
- If the stock crashes in price to $80, the investor can walk away, and the most they lose is the $1,000 paid for the option contract. That's less than the $8,000 they would have lost if they bought the 100 shares of stock.

- Also, if the stock went nowhere in price, the investor would lose the $1,000 paid for the option due to time decay. Please note: Call options are useless unless the stock increases in price.

In summary, call options allow investors to place cheap bets that a stock will rise in price without buying the stock upfront. Yet, people say options are risky, HA! I'm just teasing. I know why people say options are risky. They are referring to *'trading options.'* Yes, trading options can be risky if you misuse them, but if you prudently use them like Warren Buffett, you should be fine.

Lastly, if you want to buy call options, you'll need a brokerage account with permission to buy options contracts. Every brokerage has different criteria for approval, but the factors in their decision will include your experience as an investor and how much money you have in your account.

My Favorite Stock for Call Options

I primarily buy calls of an index, but here are a few definitions to help you understand. An **index** is a measure or method to track the performance of a group of assets. In the case of the Standard and Poor's 500 (S&P 500), it's an index that tracks the performance of the 500 strongest companies trading in the U.S. markets. It's often used to gauge the stock market's overall health or performance.

An **index fund** is a mutual fund or ETF that seeks to replicate the performance of an index, often by holding the same stocks as the index itself. More specialized indexes also track a particular industry or segment of the overall stock market. However, I don't use those. I prefer to use broad-based indexes that capture the entire stock market as a whole. Lastly, an **exchange-traded fund, or ETF,** is built like a mutual fund but can be bought or sold throughout the day like a stock.

Now back to why I'm sharing this . . .

You may remember the Buffett call if you read *Options Trading Made Simple.* If you did not read that book, it's a call option that expires two to three years out in time, and I call it the Buffett call because I modeled it after Warren Buffett's long-term options approach. The Buffett call is part of the enhanced buy & hold blueprint; now you can see how I integrate it into my overall portfolio. The Buffett call can technically be used on any stock, but I prefer using an index or exchange-traded fund (ETF) that tracks or mirrors the performance of the S&P 500 index.

As a trader, if I want to buy and hold shares of the S&P 500, one of the vehicles I can do this through is the ETF with the stock symbol: SPY (again, it's often pronounced as S.P.Y. or spy). It's a low-cost way to get exposure to the entire stock market. Another benefit of SPY that I didn't discover until later in my career is that it can handle "size."

Meaning you won't have to adjust your approach once you start trading with a six- or seven-figure account.

SPY is also not actively managed, meaning no one is trying to pick stock winners each year. The stocks in the ETF either meet the criteria or they don't. If a company in the index fails, it's replaced with another winner. I love it! Someone passively manages it for me and ensures I only invest in the winning companies that pass a strict criterion.

Also, broad-based ETFs like SPY are more diversified and have less risk and volatility than individual stocks. This stability helps my performance be more consistent and predictable. A stock can drop 20% in one day. It's much rarer to see the S&P 500 or the exchange-traded fund (SPY) drop that much in one day. At most, they may drop 5%. So those are a few reasons I only use SPY for this blueprint. Now let me share the rules I follow for the call option portion of the enhanced buy & hold portfolio.

MY RULES FOR THE BUFFETT CALL OPTION

The Buffett call is a simple trade I place once a year, and it takes 10 minutes to set up. It's a random entry trade, meaning I can set this up anytime and in any market environment. No market timing is involved, and I don't even have to look at a stock chart to place the trade.

- I only <u>buy</u> LEAPS® or long-term options. They are options with expirations longer than a year. They are also called *'Long-Term Equity Anticipation Securities.'*
- I choose the farthest-dated December expiration available. It's usually two to three years out in time.
- I buy the call with a strike price at, or up to 10% higher than the stock price.
- I risk or invest roughly 10 to 20% of my total account value into the calls, but ultimately, it depends on how many stock shares I own.

Regardless of when I open my <u>first</u> call trade, I do an annual reset/rebalance of my portfolio at the end of the current year or the beginning of the following year. Resetting means I sell my old call options and buy a new set following the above rules. I then rinse and repeat every year, but I hold my call options for a little over a year for tax reasons.

<u>Please note</u>: Once you review the enhanced buy & hold case study, you will see these rules in action, and they will make more sense.

My Call Management Rules

- There is zero management of the trade during the year. I set it up and leave it alone. I only manage it when it's time to do my portfolio's annual reset/rebalance.
- I've never experienced a series of back-to-back LEAP call losses, but if I did, I'd either quit the strategy or replenish the account with more cash to start over.
- In regard to the EBH portfolio, I never 'exercise' the rights of my call option contract. Meaning I never use the call option to buy the stock. I only buy the calls for the leveraged return they provide (more on this in a bit).

I buy the longer-dated options because they are less affected by time decay and cheaper on an average cost basis. I reset every year for three primary reasons:

1. To capture any profit I may have before the market takes it away from me.
2. So that rapid time decay of the option is never a concern for me, and . . .
3. It allows me to rebalance my portfolio, so my allocations don't get out of whack.

<u>Please note</u>: In my taxable account, I wait for a year to pass before I manage my options positions. This helps me

take advantage of the lower tax rates for long-term capital gains. In my tax-advantaged retirement accounts, this is not a concern.

Now if all of the above rules made sense to you, good; you understand options. However, if the above sounded like a foreign language to you, no worries; it's a typical experience for beginners.

Options are a foreign concept to many. They are simple in principle but challenging to understand at first. I was dazed and confused for about six months when I started learning about options. I honestly felt stupid and wondered if others were as confused as I was. However, my mentor made millions with options, so I was determined to master this topic. Over time, as you continue to study, things will slowly start to make sense. Just be patient with yourself.

When you profit and earn returns that people think are too good to be true, you'll be glad you decided not to give up. Regarding returns, let's examine the pros and cons of using call options in various market conditions.

HOW CALLS WORK IN BULL AND BEAR MARKETS

For reference, a bull market means stocks are consistently rising in price over a long period of time. And a bear market is when stocks consistently fall in price over a long period.

The trade below was covered previously, but since this chapter is about calls, I want to show it again, so you can see that calls are both good and bad depending on how the market behaves. I'll also compare the overall performance of the call options to buy & hold.

Round One: January 14, 2021 to January 18, 2022

- The ETF SPY rises in price from $378.46 to $456.49, a 20.6% gain.
- The December 2023, 380 call option rises in price from $48.77 to $104.29, a 113.8% gain.

I want to focus on the 113.8% gain, which is why we buy call options. This high return seems too good to be true until you realize it always happens in real estate. Buying options, as well as purchasing investment property, give us leverage. Leverage is just a fancy way of describing a method of buying something big for very little money. You pay a small deposit or premium upfront, then you get to control one hundred percent of the asset.

Again, with call options, we will never 'exercise' the rights of our option contracts so we can buy the stock. We only purchase the calls for the leveraged return they provide. Think real estate investing; it allows you to build wealth without buying the house for personal use. You only put down a small amount of money, but you have access to and can benefit from the asset going up in value. You are buying the house as an investment because of the leverage it can provide. You never intend to own it for personal use.

Now back to options . . .

The above call option gives us the right to buy 100 shares of SPY @ $380, and we paid $4,877 for this, right. We control $38,000 worth of stock for a fraction of the cost of buying 100 shares.

During the year, the stock rose in price from $378.46 to $456.49. A $78 increase in price, or a 20% gain in one year. If we wanted to capture the profit, we could exercise the rights of the call, buy the stock, and then sell it for a profit. Of course, we'd need $38,000 to do that. However, there is a cheaper alternative to capturing the profit. You sell the option contract to capture your profit.

We own a contract that says we can buy a $456 asset for only $378. Do you think that contract is now more valuable than the $4K we paid? Yes, it is, and the higher the stock rises, the more valuable the call contract becomes. Depending on which option you buy, it often moves almost dollar for dollar with the stock price. So that call option you purchased would also increase in price close to the $78 the stock increased in price. You saw this with the call we bought. It grew in price from $48.77 to $104.29. That's a $55.52 gain, but since we only have to put up $48.77, the gain equals a 113.8% return on our money.

If you're lost on the math, no worries; the main goal is to show you that we can use calls to make big profits. Then we can sell the option to capture the gain without coughing up thousands of dollars to buy the stock. It's an example of the leverage of options. A small amount of money controls and benefits from a bigger asset. That's one of two reasons we buy these calls. The second reason will be revealed in the next chapter.

People keep saying that trading options is risky, but we are doing what real estate investors have done for years. We are investing small amounts of money to control and benefit from a large asset. In the case of call options, the asset is stock shares. Now let's do an option reset (buy new options with a farther-dated expiration) and then see what happens when the asset drops in price.

Round Two: January 18, 2022 to January 19, 2023

- SPY stock declines in price from $456.49 to $388.64, a -14.9% loss.
- The December 2024, 460 call option declines in price from $65.50 to $21, a -67.9% loss.

As you can see, call options do great when the market goes up. But when the market falls, calls get destroyed. That's leverage in reverse.

Call Option Summary

Call options allow you to make (or lose) money from stock price movement without buying stocks.

- The average buy & return over the two years was a positive 2.85%.
- The average call option return over the two years was a positive 24.45%.

Even with the massive loss, the average call option return is still ahead percentagewise compared to buy & hold. However, options are leveraged investing vehicles, so it's unfair to compare them to buy & hold directly. That's the mistake I and many others have made before. We look at the numbers and make decisions based on the numbers. However, the real world is not lived inside of a spreadsheet. Don't make the mistake of removing the emotional factor from the numbers.

Chasing after the high returns without considering the impact it will have on your emotions is a catastrophic mistake. Logically, people will choose to earn a 24% return over a 2% return, but that comparison is made based on greed. If you haven't heard, being a greedy investor will eventually cause you to go broke.

<u>Here is my blunt warning</u>: Call options can give you super performance but can also cause you to lose ALL your money!

Also, the above-average numbers don't factor in the worst-case scenario. For example, the option contract lost 67.9% of its value in one year. What if the market went down for three years straight like it did from 2000–2002? You'd lose on buy & hold, but not 100% of your money, and you could also wait until the SPY stock shares recovered in price since the shares don't have an expiration date.

With the call option, however, you'd lose 100% of your investment due to leverage working in reverse. Also, the option has an expiration date. It disappears and ceases to exist after a certain amount of time. If you don't make money during the call options shelf life, you lose 100% of your investment due to time decay. The thought of losing 100% of your investment should scare you!

Of course, since we only allocate a small portion of our account to calls, a 100% loss would only put about a 10% dent in our overall account. Knowing exactly how much damage can happen to my account is more comforting than having 100% of my money at the mercy of the whims of buy & hold. Regardless, you should be careful with buying call options. If misused, they can be financially devastating. I'll share a real-life example of that next.

4

WHY INVESTORS FAIL WHEN
THEY BUY CALL OPTIONS

A smart man makes a mistake, learns from it, and never makes that mistake again. But a wise man finds a smart man and learns from him how to avoid the mistake altogether.

— ROY H. WILLIAMS

If you study options trading for any length of time, you will stumble across experts who will tell you not to 'buy' options but instead 'sell' them. Then they will spread lies and misinformation about how buying options doesn't work. They may mean well, but they are wrong, and if you listen to them, you won't achieve the results profiled in this book. Also, remember the earlier lesson about being an either or thinker? Don't think of option buying versus option selling. Think both. Learn both methods as I did, implement the best of each approach, and get the best of both worlds.

Now let me share two common reasons why investors fail when buying options: time in the trade and emotions.

Do you want to increase your chances of having success with buying options? If so, buy LEAP or long-term options, not short-term ones. Most people new to options trading will buy options that expire in three months or less, mainly because they are cheaper. However, predicting what the stock market will do in three months is nearly impossible. Thus, with LEAP options, we avoid having to predict. Instead, we model successful buy & hold investors and focus on the stock market's long-term trend.

Second, let's talk about emotions. My experience as a coach has taught me that the one variable that prevents most from achieving stock market success is emotions. It's the number one profit killer!

Emotions manifest themselves in several ways, but the two most common are fear and greed. More specifically, the greed of wanting more and wanting it quickly and the fear of losing what we have or losing more of what we have. Greed often causes people to invest more aggressively, and they lose the money they make. And fear often prevents people from actually investing, or if they do, they don't take the necessary risk to grow the account.

Here is an example of how this plays out in real life . . .

In 2019, I was trading with a group of investors, and we were using the Buffett call option. The stock market was raging higher, and we were achieving profits that experts would say were too good to be true. More specifically, we doubled our money on those call positions every four to six months.

Making that much money so fast caused one of the traders in the group to get greedy. Thus in 2020, coming off the previous year's profit high, this investor increased their call allocation to 50% of their account. If you read my earlier book, *Options Trading Made Simple*, you already know how I feel about this; it's dumb! Anyone who does this doesn't appreciate their money and will soon lose it. Money only stays with and gravitates toward people who steward it properly.

Preaching aside, the market crashed in March of 2020, and that investor lost so much money on those calls that they freaked out and closed them. What about the rest of the group? Since we only had 10–20% of our account allocated to those calls, we could withstand the terror of the rapid decline. At the end of 2020, when the market finally recovered, we cashed out our positions for over a 100% gain.

So, we made money, but **greed** caused one investor in the group to lose nearly 40% of the value of their account.

Fear is a cousin of greed, so let's see how fear infects investors' minds.

At the beginning of 2021, when it was time to buy a new set of Buffett calls, do you think this wayward investor joined us? Think about it, we used the same 'strategy' but had vastly different results because of emotions. One investor lost roughly 40% of their account, and the rest of us were able to double our money. I think you know the answer. This investor did <u>not</u> join us in 2021 because they were too scared.

Near the end of 2021, when we were cashing out yet another gain, I checked in with this investor to see if they were celebrating with us. I was disheartened to hear they didn't even buy any new calls. When I asked why, they said they didn't trust the market. They thought it might fall again because we were still in a pandemic. They didn't want to lose any more money. That's **fear** on display.

So, there you go! That was a real-life example of how fear and greed rear its ugly head in an investor's life. Strategies are rarely ever the real issue holding you back financially. It's usually our flawed human nature that gets in the way.

Lastly, after years of buying call options, I learned how to benefit from calls without going broke because of their downfalls. There are two ways I achieve this, 1) I invest a small amount of my account in call options, or 2) I balance the risk of calls with put options (or puts for short). Puts are what we will cover in the next chapter. See you there.

5

LIVING FREE FROM THE WORRY OF STOCK MARKET CRASHES

Unless you can watch your stock holding decline by 50% without becoming panic-stricken, you should not be in the stock market.

— WARREN BUFFETT

I don't know Mr. Buffett personally, but I have read that he has a similar emotional temperament to me regarding money. We don't get bothered by investment losses. But then again, maybe it's because we are following a plan and know the statistical probability of it working out. We are investing with logic, not emotions. Regardless, the above quote is rather blunt and can make people feel like they shouldn't invest if they feel normal emotions.

I'm a unique individual; I get that. Said another way, I'm not normal. My wife agrees. Most normal people would panic watching their account decline by 50%, and I don't blame you. It's scary, especially since losses happen more quickly than gains. You could have spent 20 years saving that money, and if half of it disappeared in a year, it would be terrifying.

The good news is that the tool discussed in this chapter was created to protect you against such events. It will give you peace of mind and was designed to ensure you don't have those 50% declines in your account. This tool allows you to live free from the worry of market crashes, and it's the secret to why my clients don't panic during market declines.

Even the billionaire investor, Mark Cuban, used it to protect 1.4 billion in stock he received when he sold his company (Mohamed, 2020). The tool is called a **protective put option**, or *'stock insurance'* as I often call it. Strictly speaking, there is no such thing as stock insurance. However, put options were created as a form of insurance, and this is arguably, one of the most important aspects of the enhanced buy & hold blueprint.

PUT OPTION BASICS

Again, options are relatively unknown to most stock market investors and are considered risky. Ironically, options were created to protect investors from risk. In the case of put options, they were created so investors could buy insurance for their stock investments to prevent losing large sums of money. Put option contracts are the opposite of call options, but they still have some of the same standardized features.

- A person who **buys one put option** has the right, but not the obligation, to sell 100 shares of stock, at a set price, on or before a specific date.
- Again, options are contracts between two parties. So if you exercised your rights, the seller of the put would be obligated to buy the shares you wanted to sell.
- When the rights of the option contract are exercised, the price the stock can be sold at is the **option's strike price**.
- Since you are buying an insurance contract, you have to pay a small fee known as the **premium**. Option premiums, or prices, are always listed as small numbers, but since the option contract controls 100 shares of stock, you have to multiply the premium by 100 to get the trust cost of buying the option.
- The contract also has an **expiration** date and is only valid for a certain period of time.
- Because of the limited shelf life, the options suffer from a concept called **time decay**. A small portion of the option's value is lost each day that passes.

To buy put options, you'll need the same brokerage account permissions as you do with buying call options.

Now let's revisit the hypothetical example from the previous chapter, but this time it will be in reverse because, again, put option benefits are the opposite of call option benefits. Call options allow an investor to place a small bet on a stock's price movement without coughing up thousands of dollars. With a protective put, however, the investor has already purchased the stock and wants to insure their investment.

Let's say an investor buys 100 shares of stock XYZ @ $160 a share price. It would cost $16,000. If the stock went up in price, they would make money. However, if the stock falls in price, they could lose all $16,000. Investors who are nervous about losing so much money could buy insurance. They could buy a three-year 160 strike put option on stock XYZ for $10 (or $1,000). Because of the rights of the put contract, it will increase in value as the stock falls in price (and vice versa).

- Suppose the investor gets lucky, and the stock increases to $190. In this case, the protective put was unnecessary, and the investor lost the $1,000 paid for the insurance. I consider that a small price to pay for the peace of mind of being fully insured.
- However, suppose the company runs into trouble, and the stock decreases in price to $80 a share, or a 50% decline. The investor could exercise their rights of the put contract and sell the stock for

$160. Yup, even though the stock has fallen by 50%, the investor can sell it for the same price they bought it for. The only money the investor lost was the $1,000 it cost to buy the put insurance. That's much less than the $8,000 they would have lost if they didn't have stock insurance.

- And just like with calls, if the stock went nowhere in price, the investor would lose the $1,000 paid for the put option due to time decay. Please note: Puts are only helpful when stocks fall in price.

In summary, protective put options allow investors to insure their stock purchases like people buy homes and insure them. After all, if you invest hundreds of thousands of dollars to buy an asset, you might as well pay a small premium to have complete protection against a massive loss. Something I wish someone would have told Betty to do. It's a sad story that we will cover in the next chapter. It illustrates why I'm such a big proponent of buying put options. Now, let's discuss the rules I follow for the put option portion of the enhanced buy & hold portfolio.

MY RULES FOR THE PROTECTIVE PUT OPTION (AKA STOCK INSURANCE)

I have good news. The rules for my puts are the same as the call options. Here they are again, so you don't have to revisit the previous chapter: Buying a protective put is a simple trade I place once a year, and it takes 10 minutes to set up. It's a random entry trade, meaning I can set this up anytime and in any market environment. There is no market timing involved, and I always buy my protective put options at the same time I buy my call options.

- I only <u>buy</u> LEAPS® or long-term options. They are options with expirations longer than a year. They are also called *'Long-Term Equity Anticipation Securities.'*
- I choose the farthest-dated December expiration available. It's usually two to three years out in time.
- I buy the put that has a strike price at, or up to 10% higher than the stock price.
- I risk or invest roughly 10 to 20% of my total account value into the puts, but ultimately, it depends on how many stock shares I own.

Regardless of when I open my <u>first</u> put trade, I will sell it at the end of the current year or the beginning of the following year, and then I will buy a new put following the above rules. This is the annual reset/rebalance of my portfolio. I hold this next put for a little over a year and then sell it. Afterward, I rinse and repeat every single year. And again, you will see these rules in action during the enhanced buy & hold case study.

My Put Management Rules

- There is zero management of the trade during the year. I set it up and leave it alone. I only manage it when it's time to do the annual reset/rebalance of the portfolio.
- With protective puts, **I expect and am okay with a series of back-to-back LEAP put losses**. If that happens, it means the market <u>did not crash</u>, and that's ultimately what I want.
- In regard to the EBH portfolio, I never 'exercise' the rights of my put option contract to sell the stock. I only buy the puts for peace of mind and to offset any losses I experience during market crashes.

I buy the longer-dated options because they are less affected by time decay and cheaper on an average cost basis. I reset every year for three primary reasons:

1. The stock market goes up more than it goes down, so if I ever have profit on my puts, I want to capture it before the market goes back up in price.
2. I don't want rapid time decay of the option ever to be a concern for me. And . . .
3. It allows me to rebalance my portfolio, so my allocations don't get out of whack.

<u>Please note</u>: In my taxable account, I wait for a year to pass before I manage my options positions. This helps me take advantage of the lower tax rates for long-term capital gains. In my tax-advantaged retirement accounts, this is not a concern.

HOW PUTS WORK IN BULL AND BEAR MARKETS

For the EBH portfolio, I am not 'trading' puts. This means I am not trying to time the market and profit from declining stocks. The purpose of puts in the EBH portfolio is to replace the need for bonds. Meaning their sole purpose is to stabilize my portfolio during market declines. The downfall is that the puts drag down my overall performance in up markets. I can live with this tradeoff because protective puts make money in down markets, which helps stabilize my emotions during market crashes.

For example, during the market decline of 2020, the stock market fell nearly 30% in just a few weeks. It freaked so many people out that they panic-sold their stocks. Not my clients, though; they all had put options in place. Here is a note I received from one of them:

> *"I got the best night's sleep that I've had in a long time. I didn't care whether the market went up or down."*
>
> — JOHN

It's excellent receiving notes like this but getting folks on board with the concept of buying puts for insurance was a painful process. It took much convincing, and even once they bought the puts, they would constantly complain. Why? Because people hate buying something that constantly loses money. You'll see what I mean in the following examples. We'll use the 2021 to 2023 case study profiled in the call option chapter.

Round one: January 14, 2021 to January 18, 2022

- SPY stock rises in price from $378.46 to $456.49, a 20.6% gain.
- The December 2023, 380 put option declines in price from $59.35 to $28.18, a -52.5% loss.

As you can see, it sucks to own put options when the market goes up. And guess what? The market goes up more than down, so I usually lose money on the puts in my accounts. However, during the rare times the market does fall, the puts give me comfort because it feels good seeing something make money in my account during market declines.

Before we move on, let me answer one of the most common questions I get: *"Travis, since the puts lose so much money in up markets, can't we wait until the market falls to buy them?"* Sure, that's a great plan, in theory, but let me ask you this. Can you predict when you will get in a car accident, so you wait to buy insurance before that happens? It seems silly when you think about it that way. Put options are disaster insurance, and since we can't predict when the market will fall, it's best to have them in place at all times. Now let's see how puts behave in down markets.

Round two: January 18, 2022 to January 19, 2023

- SPY stock declines in price from $456.49 to $388.64, a -14.9% loss.
- The December 2024, 460 put option increases in price from $64.50 to $74, a 14.7% gain.

So in a down market, puts make money and provide peace of mind. However, put options are not a perfect solution, and their gain usually doesn't cover 100% of the losses you experience on your stock shares. This is another thing clients struggle with. They expect to see the puts offset their losses on a dollar-for-dollar basis, which is usually not the case.

The real benefits of puts are only seen in severe crashes of 30–50%, but that's also when they are most needed. Those are the emotionally triggering kinds of declines that are impossible to predict. Thus, it's best to always have protective puts in place just in case of a severe crash. Just like it's best to have homeowners' insurance just in case your house catches on fire.

Regardless of if your puts fully recoup the loss you take on the stock, it's nice to have them in place for the peace of mind factor. That benefit alone is priceless, and it's hard to put a value on it. As a coach, I have noticed that the investors who own protective puts are less emotionally reactive to stocks falling in price. They don't freak out and sell their stocks because they have fallen in price. That said, let's wrap this up with a summary.

Put Option Summary

- The average buy & return over the two years was a positive 2.85%.
- The average put option return over the two years was a negative 18.9%.

So yes, puts costs money and hinders your portfolio's performance, but come on, isn't the peace of mind and market crash protection worth it? If you're shaking your head, no, I understand. I've been coaching for nearly two decades and have not met a client who was 'okay' with less-than-average returns. Thus, I had to teach them the solution to this problem. We discussed it in the previous chapter; it's call options. Do you recall me stating that I balance the risk of call options with put options?

Here is what I mean. If you take the average call option performance from the last chapter (+24.45%) and subtract it from the average put performance we just discussed (-18.9%), you get a positive 5.55%.

So again, the puts drag down your performance, but success with investing is more than just about making the most money. It's also about what's best for you emotionally. Emotions are what cause people to underperform and encounter losses. Studies have proven that you will do better if you hold stocks and don't sell during down periods (Stevens, 2021). However, people still sell despite overwhelming data that it's a bad idea to sell. Why? Emotions.

Emotions are more influential than logic. Thus, we are trying to create a system to bypass our emotional triggers. Emotions can also blind people to beautiful truths right in front of their faces. For example, most people always point out that they could make more money if they didn't own the puts. However, even with the put dragging down the performance, you still would have earned a positive 5.55% return.

With that return, you still beat the average buy & return of 2.85% during the same period, but you also got the best of both worlds. You achieved a bit of super performance, but you were also protected from market crashes. **The subdued put + call return means you never make so much that it causes you to be greedy, and you also never lose so much that it causes you to panic.** It's truly a genius system that I was blessed to stumble across.

Now that we have covered put options, let me share the structure of enhanced buy & hold (or EBH for short). The EBH portfolio is comprised of the following:

1. Call options for super performance <u>AND</u> to pay for the puts.
2. Traditional buy & hold, i.e., passive index fund/ETF investing for long-term passive wealth building. And . . .
3. Put options for market crash protection and peace of mind.

It's a relatively simple setup, but don't let the simplicity fool you. Too often, people make investing unnecessarily complicated, believing that complexity equals profit. Sometimes, success means making things so simple that you can't help but succeed. For example, using the results of the mini case studies, let's see how powerful this simple setup is:

- The average call option performance from the last chapter (+24.45%).
- The average buy & hold return (+2.85%). And . . .
- This chapter's average put option performance (-18.9%).

If you combine all three returns, the average return is 8.4%, nearly three times the return of the pure buy & hold approach. So, in my not-so-humble opinion, **you just**

discovered how to rapidly build wealth while living free from the worry of market crashes. Of course, we don't invest our entire account in options, but you can see how the options boost our account. It enhances our performance. Before we move on, I want to be clear about something . . .

Enhanced buy & hold is not a magic pill or a quick path to riches. It does require study and practice on your end. It's an approach designed to empower you to build wealth using professional tools, strategies, and guidance. It's a simple blueprint, but it's certainly not easy. When you first learn it, it can seem overwhelming and complicated. However, you'll see it's a simple set-it-and-forget-it system once you push through the initial nervousness and discomfort. For most clients, the hardest part is managing their emotions of fear and greed. In my experience, success with money is 80% mental and 20% technical know-how. And in the next chapter, you'll see a tragic example of how emotions can be the number one profit killer for investors.

6

WHY YOU NEED TO BUY STOCK INSURANCE

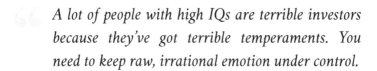

A lot of people with high IQs are terrible investors because they've got terrible temperaments. You need to keep raw, irrational emotion under control.

— CHARLIE MUNGER

Before I talk about Betty, a quick intro and a backstory. It is generally accepted that traditional buy & hold with index funds can make you rich. If so, why do 'average' people fail with traditional buy & hold? It's because with buy & hold, we have no insurance. We put ourselves in a position to lose a great deal of money in a market crash, and we don't like the pain of losing lots of money. We view it as a punishment versus a fee we pay to participate in the gains of the stock market.

It's also unwise to put yourself in a position to lose all your money without any insurance or protection in place. We know this at an instinctual level, but we often don't have the tools to do anything about it. Or either we don't know that the tools exist. Sadly, the tool to prevent stock market losses has existed since the 1970s. It's called a stock option. More specifically, protective put options.

So again, yes, buy & hold works, mathematically and historically. You can get rich following the standard buy & hold wisdom if you stay steadfast and don't deviate from it. And that's the flaw. Staying steadfast when losing money does not align with how most people's brains are wired. This is plainly illustrated through Betty's story . . .

I was at a church dinner party, and we were doing intros and icebreakers. One of the guests asked a variation of the following question: *"If money wasn't a factor, what would you choose to do as a career?"* I'm a hardcore introvert and generally a shy person. Thus, I was the last to answer. I was also hesitant to give my answer, and you are about to see why . . .

I was the only person at the table who replied with: *"I'd do exactly what I'm doing right now."* As expected, I got looks of both envy and disgust. However, one brave lady, who wasn't busy hating on me, asked me what I did for a living. Ugh, I hate that question, and here is why . . .

1. It's difficult to explain what I do for a living (I trade options).
2. I achieved financial freedom at 34, and people older than me who are still working in corporate America generally hate hearing about all my personal freedom. And . . .
3. Most people don't understand the stock market.

Regardless, I usually reply to that type of question with something like: *"I'm an investment educator. I help people understand stock market investing."* The replies to that vary, but here was the reply this night. She said, *"Oh, the stock market! To be honest, I don't understand investing, and now I'm scared to invest because my mom lost all of her money in the stock market."*

Of course, that piqued my interest, so I politely asked her to elaborate. The following story she shared broke my heart, and it's one of the many reasons I now write these kinds of books. It's selfish for me to keep this information to myself while people like Betty suffer due to a lack of knowledge. Here is her story . . .

To protect her privacy, I am calling her Betty, and she was a recent widow. Her husband, the sole income earner in the house, passed away in 2007. Like most Americans, they lived paycheck to paycheck and found it hard to save on the little income they brought in. Thus, Betty had little to no retirement or personal savings when her husband died.

Lucky for her, there was a life insurance policy. The money she received from the policy was all she had. She had to pay her bills, and the money needed to last long enough to take care of her for the rest of her life.

So let me stop here and ask you to empathize with Betty. Your significant other has recently passed away. You're most likely grieving and can't think at an optimal level. You've also never had a large sum of money before, and you have no clue what to do with it. So what do you think someone like Betty would do—aside from consulting family and friends?

Would she buy a book like this one to learn how to manage money? No! There is no time for that. Her problem is immediate and pressing, and she fears she might make a mistake and lose all the money. That's a risk she can't afford to take. So, she does what many in her situation do; she goes to a financial advisor, usually a local one in her hometown.

I'm unclear on 'who' told Betty to put most of the money into the stock market, but she did. Over time, the stock market is one of the best places to park money for long periods of time. The growth achieved would help the money last longer for Betty. In theory, it was an adequate plan, but the reality was much uglier. Remember, this was in 2007.

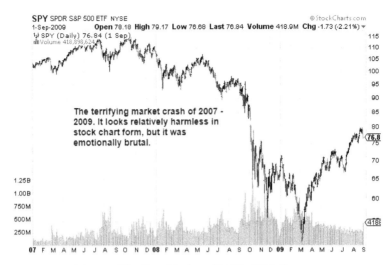

Figure 4 The Bear Market of 2007–2009, Source:
StockCharts.com

No one could have predicted how bad the market crash of 2007–2009 would be. Even the best forms of diversification didn't save people's portfolios from getting demolished. Remember, Betty has no source of income. Her husband, the sole income earner, is deceased, and she's still mourning. The financial gift her husband left her is now at risk of being wiped out. So what would you have done if you were Betty, in her vulnerable position, and watching the only money you had to your name evaporate?

Would you have held steady and not sold your stocks, as a financial advisor would recommend? Remember, most financial advisors get paid whether you make money or not. Your portfolio is 'their' cash cow, so they are motivated to keep you invested for as long as possible.

But in defense of advisors, yes, if you hold your stocks for the long term and don't sell during down markets, you will usually recover your losses. However, if you have invested for over five years, you know the flaw in that plan. It doesn't work with human nature!

Humans, by and large, hate the pain of losing money. They will do everything in their power to avoid it. Yes, a few unicorns have the emotional fortitude to watch 50% of their money disappear, and it does not bother them. But the 'average' person in Betty's situation cannot tolerate that kind of loss. The average person will not just toughen up and deal with it. Most people would go crazy, and their irrational brains would take over, and they may do something like cash out their stocks during a crash.

And usually, right after they sell to stop the pain, the market starts to go back up. Sigh! I can't tell you how often I've seen that story play out. Thus, a better method than buy and pray is buy and insure. We are already programmed to buy insurance for cars and homes, so buying insurance for stocks takes advantage of programming that is already in place.

But Betty, like most, didn't even know that you could insure your stock portfolio. Worse than that, most financial advisors aren't allowed to use puts to protect their client's portfolios. Don't even get me started on how backward that is. You manage money for a living, but industry regulations prevent you from buying insurance for your client's accounts (shaking my head).

Anyhow . . .What do you think Betty did?

Yup, she freaked out and cashed out in early 2009, right when the market was bottoming and about to go higher. It would continue to go up for the next 13 years. If Betty didn't cash out, she would have been okay. But since none of us can predict the future, she made what she thought was the best choice at the time—salvage what little money she had left. I don't know if Betty got back into the stock market, but I doubt it. I swear, I almost cried hearing that story. I hate seeing elders suffer.

Maybe I can't save the Bettys of the world, but hopefully, I can reach their kids or loved ones. Maybe you can develop the skills necessary to manage money successfully. Then you can help the Bettys of your family. Let's commit to making the world a better place for our aging population who missed out on all this knowledge. Betty losing that much money, and having that kind of experience, was utterly unnecessary and didn't need to happen. But how do we prevent this from happening to us?

- We do it by finding a way to invest that doesn't trigger our emotions.
- We find a method where the max we can lose in any crash is so small that we won't be triggered emotionally.

- More specifically, we find a way to make money when markets crash.

If you look at your portfolio during a bear market and see that you are making money, would you be tempted to cash out all of your investments? Uh, no, because you would not need to. And the best tool I have found that accomplishes all the above is put options. And now that we have covered puts, let's move on to discuss what I use for the buy & hold component of the EBH portfolio.

7

THE SIMPLEST PATH TO WEALTH

If investing is entertaining, if you're having fun, you're probably not making any money. Good investing is boring.

— GEORGE SOROS

I've studied wealthy people since the early 90s and achieved financial freedom at 34 years old. At this point, I've invested well over $100,000 in courses, coaches, and seminars to learn the 'secrets' of the rich. And you know what? It was worth it! The information helped me become a first-generation millionaire. However, I discovered an ugly truth that most product promoters don't tell you. Well, several truths, actually.

1. There really are no 'secrets.' The concept of secrets will sell courses because, let's face it, we're suckers for information that we think will give us an advantage over our investment peers.
2. There is no one ideal path. There are hundreds of ways to get rich (gasp). And . . .
3. You can charge more for a complicated strategy, but the more complicated something is, the more chances you will screw it up. Complicated strategies make you feel smart, but simple elementary strategies usually make the most money in the long run. At least, that has been my experience.

So, after much research and studying wealth for over two decades, I want to share the simplest path to stock market wealth I have ever discovered. Please note that I didn't say it's the best or the most profitable. I said it's the simplest. And you know what? I have discovered that the simpler something is, the more success I have with it. Without any further delay, here is the plan . . .

My family follows what I call a one-stock retirement plan. I discovered one stock that provides income and adequate growth and keeps the risk of losing our money as low as possible. Why would I invest my money elsewhere if I could get all those benefits from one stock? Even Warren Buffett, one of the world's most famous investors, often recommends that people put their money into this one investment (Locke, 2021/2022). So, who am I to argue with the wisdom of a billionaire? Thus, our core holding is the S&P 500.

The S&P 500, created in 1926, tracks the rise and fall of the 500 largest stocks trading on U.S. exchanges. The S&P 500 is arguably the most critical market performance measure used by investors and traders worldwide. With just one investment, you get instant exposure to the entire market at a low cost. However, there is one hiccup.

You can't directly buy the S&P 500. But you can invest in its alternative, SPDR S&P 500 ETF Trust (stock symbol: SPY). It's an exchange-traded fund (ETF) that tracks the S&P 500. Broad-based ETFs, like SPY, are more diversified and have less risk and volatility than individual stocks. Individual stocks concentrate my risk of loss into one company. However, SPY spreads my risk of loss across 500 companies.

SPY is also the oldest and one of the most heavily traded ETFs. So if you're looking for an excellent investment, it's hard to beat the S&P 500. Do you want to own the top tech stocks? How about the leading consumer brands? Maybe you want to own whatever sector is the hottest right now. Yes, those are all in the S&P 500, and when you buy it, you instantly own the best stocks in the U.S. economy.

It's also hard to screw up a one-stock S&P 500 retirement plan. Even my wife, who hates thinking about investing, can follow that. The conversation went something like this: *"Hey honey, from now on, we will put all of our money into the S&P 500 through SPY or our Vanguard S&P 500 mutual fund. If I die, and you get life insurance, dump it into the S&P 500 and forget about it."* She replied, "Sounds good to me!" and then moved on with her life.

Now consider if I told her this: *"Hey honey, dump 60% of our money into Fund A, 10% into Fund B, 12% into Fund C, and another 18% into Fund D. And oh, don't forget to rebalance each year if things get out of whack."*

There are so many potential problems with the more complicated approach that I don't even have time to get into them in this book. First, my wife, who hates math, needs to break out a calculator to get the allocation percentages correct. Then, my wife, who is extremely scatterbrained and overstimulated by our children's requests, has to remember to rebalance each year. This is the same woman who doesn't even know her login ID to her retirement account. That's how infrequently she looks at it.

And no, I'm not talking about my wife behind her back. I'm not that stupid, ha-ha. I had her approve these comments (smile).

In theory, my wife can handle a complicated investment strategy, but I live in a world of reality, and I know she needs simplicity. Thus, I switched all my accounts to this simple one-stock blueprint. As a savvy investor, I can handle a complicated strategy and would do fine. However, I won't live forever, and I don't want my wife to inherit a big mess of confusion she has no idea how to handle.

Now we focus on a single stock; it's like owning an apartment building with 500 individual units managed by someone else. We no longer have to stress about a lousy company earnings report. We have saved hundreds of hours because we don't have to research individual company stocks extensively. There is no single company bankruptcy risk. And the SPY ETF collects the dividends issued by all the dividend-paying stocks in the S&P 500 and sends that money to us.

The SPY ETF has become the ultimate *set it and forget it* stock we can hold forever and even pass down to our kids. More importantly, SPY has listed options to trade. That means with just one stock . . .

- We can achieve growth through call options and stock price appreciation.
- We can generate income through stock dividends and option selling strategies.
- We can obtain market crash protection through put options.

Growth, income, and market crash protection—it's the trifecta of wealth building. For us, there are more pros than cons to using this one stock blueprint. And again, it's also the simplest path to wealth I have ever encountered. This style of investing is also known as index fund investing. And with that said, I have a confession . . .

I have to give credit where credit is due. Guess who I learned this simple investing strategy from? The same buy & hold bigots I talked about in a previous chapter. I learned several of my most profitable insights from buy & hold bigots, and one is the benefits of investing in broad-based index funds.

Index fund investing is not exciting, but it can make you rich. Studies even show that the large majority of actively managed funds fail to beat the performance of the S&P 500 (Coleman, 2023). That's a simple truth I learned from the buy & hold investors I used to ridicule and make fun of. Now I appreciate them because I have learned a ton and made more money because of their wisdom. So yeah, I gave them a hard time earlier in the book, but I agree with them to an extent.

I don't believe 'average people' can consistently beat the stock market's performance, nor should they try to. Ninety percent of the population (the average investor) should adopt a simple buy & hold approach using low-cost index funds. If you do that, you'll outperform the majority of your peers. Said another way, invest as average people do if you want average results. But consider this, being an average investor is a choice. You can also choose to be an above-average investor and put in the work necessary to develop those skills. That said, let's talk about the rules I follow . . .

MY RULES FOR THE ETF BUY & HOLD SHARES

- I break all the rules of traditional diversification and put roughly 80% of my account into the S&P 500 through the ETF SPY. The other 20% of my account will be devoted to call and put options on SPY.
- No matter how many shares I own, I will always have the shares paired up with SPY call and put options. I follow a 1:1 ratio.

1:1 ratio example: Since one option contract represents 100 shares of a stock, you match the number of option contracts with the corresponding number of stock shares. So, 100 shares of stock would be paired up with one option contract. I use 50 shares as the transition point. For example. . .

- 0 to 150 shares of stock are paired up with one call option and one put option.
- 151 to 250 shares of stock are paired up with two calls and two puts.

- Etc. Etc.

My favorite part of this blueprint is that I plan on holding these shares for life! I never plan on selling them. The goal is to keep accumulating shares over time so that dividends can support our lifestyle. Any extra money we make from options will be used to buy more SPY shares. Why is that? Because it's passive income investing. We make money without lifting a finger.

The option profit, on the other hand, is active income. Yes, it's leverage returns and better than buy & hold, but it still requires me to show up to generate those profits. What if I'm making $100,000 a year as an active trader, and then I have a stroke like my brother did in his early 40s? My entire income and livelihood go bye-bye in an instant. That's a risk I used to be comfortable taking, but not anymore. His stroke freaked me out, and I saw another flaw in active trading. Active trading income depends on the best-case scenario (i.e., always being around to trade your account).

However, with buy & hold, all I have to do is 'buy' and then 'hold' for life. Another benefit of holding for life and never selling is that I will never have to pay taxes on my gains. And then, as an accountant once told me, our kids can inherit our portfolio on a stepped-up cost basis. Their cost basis for tax purposes will be the value of the stocks the day they inherited them, not the price I paid for them. However, please double-check with a qualified tax professional. I'm not an accountant, and the rules could have changed by the time you read this book.

Full disclosure: The *'plan'* is to hold them for life, but sometimes life gets messy. If we ever need money, we are not averse to selling off a bit of stock to come up with the cash, like when we gifted money to elderly family members so they could purchase their dream home.

My Buy & Hold Management Rules

- There is zero management of these shares during the year or EVER! I set it and forget it.
- When it's time to do the annual reset/rebalance of my portfolio, I don't do anything with the shares except maybe buy more. The rebalancing is for the option positions only.
- And as I accumulate more shares, I buy more calls and puts to accompany those shares.

Let me stop here in case you have the following question: *"So Travis, are you telling me to just put all of my money into the S&P 500?"*

It's a great question, and it gives me a chance to explain that I'm not a financial advisor and can't give you investment advice. I don't know the particulars of your financial situation, and the small details matter a lot. I am only an expert in what I did to rapidly build wealth, retire early, and ensure I don't lose my accumulated wealth. Thus, I take the position of an educator. I share what I do and try my best to explain all the reasonings and logic behind my decisions.

Then I share a low-risk way for you to test the concepts yourself. It's called paper or virtual trading. Paper trading is where you go through all the motions of investing, but you don't use real money. One of the many reasons you should paper trade first is because it's a cautious approach that ensures you learn how to use the tools correctly.

I don't think you should invest real money until you understand what you are doing. You don't want to lose money unnecessarily. When you're new to investing or trading options, it takes a while to master the technical aspects of it. But once you learn the mechanics, you can slowly transition to real money, where you discover how to manage the emotional part of investing.

Overcoming the fear of losing money and the greed for more is not easy at first. For this reason, it's best to tackle one skill at a time—mechanics first and emotions second. It's a more cautious and deliberate approach, and the students who follow that route tend to have a higher success rate than those who don't.

People who scoff at paper trading are often arrogant, impatient, and don't have the discipline to delay the gratification of earning real money. I'll let you guess if those character traits lead to success (wink).

That leads to another question I often get from people turned off by the simple approach of buying index funds: *"Travis, why don't you buy individual stocks? You can make more money."* Because if I buy a stock, I have created more work for myself. I must keep up with the company to ensure it remains a good investment. That means continuously monitoring the company fundamentals and paying attention to any new players that enter the market who could threaten the company's profit. This can take upwards of 10+ hours a week.

It also means I must know how to analyze a company's financials and understand terms like EBITDA to understand its earnings better. The definition of EBITDA is irrelevant to our discussion. Still, I think the average person should not invest in individual stocks unless they master what a good business looks like. However, the extra effort may not be a big deal if you're already a business owner familiar with what it takes to run a successful business.

In summary, an S&P 500 index fund is less effort than buying individual stocks. Once I buy an index fund, my job is done, and I outsource the management of it to someone else. They will do all the work of keeping track of the companies in the index, and I can sit back and enjoy my life. It saves me time, and I still win financially. So with all the great benefits of index fund investing, what are the tradeoffs?

The main one is performance. In theory, I could make more money by buying individual stocks, but I don't need to. I make up for the performance difference with call options. This way, I get the gains of a great stock investor without the hassle of investing in individual stocks. It's the same reason I no longer buy bonds. I don't need to. I use put options for protection in down markets. I'll stop here because, by now, I think you get my point. I love the simplicity of index fund investing!

Now a quick recap of what we have discussed thus far:

- You discovered how to rapidly build wealth with LEAP call options.
- You learned to invest with broad-based exchange-traded funds passively.
- And you also discovered how to use LEAP put options to protect your wealth from market crashes.

Now let's wrap up this chapter with the distinction between investing and short-term trading. All three components of the enhanced buy & hold portfolio, calls, stock shares, and puts, could be traded. What I mean by trading is buying and selling calls, puts, and stock shares on a short-term basis. It's also called market timing, and we are avoiding that with the EBH portfolio.

There are hundreds of ways to 'trade' options. And yes, with enhanced buy & hold, I am technically trading options because I close them once a year and purchase new ones. However, that's because it's a prudent way of managing the negatives of options (i.e., expiration dates, time decay, etc.). Trading once a year is a conservative approach to trading options.

We are buying and holding stocks and options. We are not actively trading stocks and options. Once the enhanced buy & hold portfolio is set up, it's left alone until a year later when it's time to rebalance it. If you want to actively trade in and out of the market, please read *Options Trading Made Simple*. That's where I covered active trading.

This book and strategy are about buying and holding. Don't miss that point! I'm trying to show you how to avoid all the costly mistakes other options traders make. And one of those mistakes is ignoring the benefit of buy & hold. Again, buy & hold is the granddaddy of all passive stock market strategies.

Think about it. Is options income truly passive? Yes and no. Yes, we generate outsized returns with little work on our part. However, options still need to be managed. They have expiration dates; we can't just set and forget them. However, with index fund investing, we can technically set it and forget it. There are no expiration dates, and the dividends are paid to us automatically.

In summary, the enhanced buy & hold portfolio is passive. It's primarily long-term investing. And with EBH, I buy an ETF that tracks the S&P 500. I then pair this up with call options and put options I buy once a year. It's simple, easy, and, best of all, it works!

8

THE ENHANCED BUY & BOLD BLUEPRINT

If you want to have a better performance than the crowd, you must do things differently from the crowd.

— JOHN TEMPLETON

E nhanced buy & hold is my 10-minute options trading and ETF investing blueprint:

- I buy shares of a broad-based index fund for safe and stable returns.
- I buy put options as a form of stock market insurance. And . . .
- I buy call options to pay for the puts and to give the account a profit boost.

And now that you have been introduced to the individual components of EBH, let's, once again tie it all together as well as share the philosophy and rationale behind it. First, I'd like to explain why this blueprint caters to people with six- and seven-figure investment accounts.

Reason #1: EBH is conservative by design and does not grow an account fast. Thus, people with small investment accounts would prefer something else.

Reason #2: If you are ever blessed enough to get to the $100,000 investment account size, you want to do everything you can to keep it from dwindling to a $10,000 account size. Thus, you use EBH to protect your account against a massive loss. Doing so also increases your chance of growing that $100K into a million-dollar account.

Reason #3: The losses on six- and seven-figure accounts trigger emotions more, and the stock insurance in this blueprint helps with that. For example, let's pretend you had an aggressive setup where $80,000 was invested in SPY shares and $20,000 in call options. Then the stock market crashed by nearly 60% like it did during the 2007–2009 market crash. Your $100,000 investment account would quickly dwindle to $30–40K. Now imagine it was a million-dollar account that dwindled to $300–400K. Not only are those tough losses to recover from financially, but your emotions would also be frazzled. You would most likely be so traumatized that you would fear getting back into the market.

Elevated emotion while you are investing money is a disaster waiting to happen. Thus, we use the puts to avoid significant losses, which helps our emotions not be triggered. The put option component of EBH is so essential. For example, I ran the numbers with the puts in place. The loss in the recently mentioned example would be a negative 14%. That is much better than the 60–70% loss with the aggressive setup.

Please note: You do not have to wait until you have a six-figure account to add the puts. You can add them sooner if you choose, but please remember that it will slow down the growth. And from my experience, people desire to get to six figures as fast as possible. At least, that was my desire. However, once our accounts grew larger and reached the six-figure mark, we scaled back on the aggressive approach to investing.

We then used EBH to ensure we kept the wealth we had built up. Of course, our portfolio stopped growing fast, but the tradeoff is that we increased our probability of keeping the money we made. And that leads to a lesson my millionaire mentor taught me about the three skill sets for building wealth (make, keep, and grow):

1. You must learn how to make money.
2. You must learn how to keep the money you make.
3. You must learn how to safely grow the money you keep.

Most people only focus on the first skill set, making money. However, you will lose all the money if you do not develop the second skill set (keeping your profits). So again, the lesson I am attempting to convey is not to be greedy.

I saw this in the cryptocurrency and NFT space. When cryptocurrencies and NFTs emerged, many people became overnight millionaires. Then most of them lost the money they made. Even if you get lucky and do not lose the money you make, you still must discover how to safely grow it into a larger pile of cash (the third skill set of building wealth). And that's where enhanced buy & hold shines. It helps you develop the second and third skill sets. That said, let's discuss how I would set up a new account.

SETTING UP A NEW PORTFOLIO

With EBH, we follow the 80/20 wealth-building formula my millionaire mentor taught me. This formula was revealed in my book *Options Trading Made Simple*. If you did not read the book, here is a summary of the formula:

Roughly 80% of your money is devoted to long-term buy & hold and 20% to short-term options trading. In a $100,000 example account, $80,000 would be used to buy shares of the S&P 500, and $20,000 would be used for short-term options trades (buying options, etc.).

With the EBH portfolio, the 20% will be used to buy a call and a put. Since buying options can be riskier than owning shares of an S&P 500 index fund, we only want to allocate a small portion of our money to options. The main goal of using options is to take advantage of the leveraged earning potential of options, but we also want to minimize the danger of losing large sums of money.

Now let's discuss the logistics of how to set up a new portfolio. If you recall from an earlier chapter, one option contract controls or represents 100 shares of stock, so you match the number of option contracts with the corresponding number of stock shares. I use 50 shares as the transition point for increasing the number of option contracts I buy.

For example:

- If I owned zero to 150 shares of stock, I would pair them up with one call option and one put option.

- If I owned 151–250 shares of stock, I would pair them up with two call options and two put options.
- Once I surpassed 250 shares, I would increase the number of option contracts to three. Then I would stick with three calls and puts until I surpassed 350 shares.

Also, this is a random entry template based on the core principles of successful buy & hold. **You can set this up at any time and in any market environment.** There is no need to time the market or get in when you think it's a good time. Waiting to enter the stock market is never good, especially with this balanced risk blueprint. The quicker you get into the market, the sooner you can take advantage of the long-term upward trend of the market.

Another critical point is that no matter if I make or lose money on my options positions, a reset/rebalance happens at the end or beginning of each year. For example, let's pretend I set up a new EBH portfolio on October 09, 2006. Because of the riskier nature of the options, I will want to reset the position in December 2006, or January 2007, to take advantage of the newer option expirations listed around those months. After this, the next reset will be one year later.

That said, here are the steps I follow to set up a new enhanced buy & hold portfolio. I will use $100,000 as an example starting amount and fictitious SPY prices. EBH is comprised of stock shares, call options, and put options. Thus, setting it up will be more expensive than just buying stock shares. First, I must find the call and put I want to purchase. Then I add up the cost of the call, the put, and one share of stock.

For example:

- $13.15 call option cost + $10.60 put option cost + $135.09 for one share of SPY = $158.84. This is my cost basis, or how much it costs to set up the enhanced buy & hold portfolio.
- I then take the amount I have available to invest and divide it by this figure.

So for the $100K portfolio we are modeling, here is what it would look like:

$100,000 divided by $159 = 628

That calculation tells me I can buy six calls, six puts, and 628 shares of stock. If I have money left over after setting this up, I either . . .

- Leave it in cash uninvested.
- Buy more calls and puts.
- Or I buy a few more shares of SPY.

A vital mindset lesson before we move on. Using those lower prices may have triggered the thought, *"Well, sure, this sounds easy when the stock price is only $135, and you can afford to buy more shares. What about now when the stock is nearly $500 a share? Your money does not go as far."*

My blunt response to that great question is: *"And, so what? My mentor called that question a loser's limp (an excuse to fail without trying). The higher stock price is an obstacle, not an excuse. Obstacles can be overcome, but excuses cannot. If you viewed the higher stock cost as an obstacle, your brain would have devised a solution. Just buy one call, one put, and however many shares you can buy. Then your goal is to keep accumulating shares until you have the required number. See, there is a solution to every obstacle. Ultimately, it doesn't matter if prices are higher now. What matters is that you get in the game. You cannot win if you stay on the sidelines making excuses as to why this will not work for you."*

With that out of the way, let us get back to the example.

After the cost basis calculation is complete and I know how many shares and options contracts to buy, I follow three simple steps. These steps can be implemented in any order, but I usually purchase the put options first. After taking care of the insurance portion, I buy the assets that help me make money, calls, and stock shares. I do it this way to train myself to focus on the risk of loss first and profits second.

Step 1: I buy the farthest-dated December LEAP put option with a strike price at, or up to 10% higher than the current stock price.

Figure 5 Setting up an order to buy six at-the-money put options, Source: Schwab.com

At-the-money (or ATM for short) means an option with a strike price closest to or at the same price as the stock. And just in case you are wondering, there is no magic about the December expiration. It's just a simple system to follow to prevent the analysis paralysis people get caught up in. Feel free to experiment with different expiration dates. However, before you tweak, I highly encourage you to succeed with how EBH is taught in this book. Earn the right to tweak.

Also, a quick reminder: I buy options with expiration dates two to three years out in time because they are cheaper on an average cost basis. For example, at the time of this writing, a one-year, at-the-money put option on SPY costs $23.59 (average cost of $1.97 a month). Logically, you would assume a two-year put would be double that price, but it is not. Instead, a two-year, at-the-money put option on SPY costs $35.50 (average cost of $1.48 a month). The reason this is the case has to do with the complicated way options are priced.

Option pricing is beyond the scope of this book. Good thing for you; you don't need to understand it to succeed with this blueprint. Said another way, the extra knowledge can help but is unnecessary. The option nerds will have an issue with my stance on this, but they can keep their opinion, and I will keep my successful results (smile). Now, let's continue to the next step.

Step 2: I buy the farthest-dated December LEAP call option with the same strike price as the put bought in Step 1. I keep the call and the put at the same strike price for simplicity reasons (Please see **Figure 5** for an example of what it looks like buying the option positions). Again, another variation I have tested is buying an option 10% higher than the stock shares. Both approaches work. However, in this book, I will model the simplest version and the one with the fewest math calculations: picking the option closest to the stock price. In option circles, this is referred to as the at-the-money option.

Speaking of simplicity, I reset the options every year, and keep the call and put at the same strike price because it is a simple system to follow. The more you simplify and systemize your investment plan, the better you will do. Why? Because most humans like to overcomplicate stuff and tinker with things. The more you tinker with your portfolio, the worse you will do. At least, that has been my experience. Your results may differ. And now, our last and final step.

Step 3: I buy shares of SPY that I plan to hold for life. There is zero trading or management of these shares. I can hold them with complete peace of mind because I bought insurance for the stock shares. Ideally, I never sell my stock shares. The ultimate goal is to accumulate enough shares so that the dividend income supports our lifestyle. Lastly, please consult your broker's tutorials if you do not know how to buy options or stock shares on their platform.

So that is how I would set up a new portfolio starting from scratch. However, if I already had a portfolio in place, I would rearrange things as needed. Now let me address a few common questions I get.

FREQUENTLY ASKED QUESTIONS

How Do You Manage the Portfolio?

I will provide the general framework I use to manage my portfolio, and then you can tailor it to fit your needs. Once the portfolio is set up, I perform a portfolio rebalance each year, where I sell the old options and buy a new set with a farther-dated expiration. If there is any money left over, more stock shares are accumulated.

If there is ever a time when I do not have enough cash to buy the needed option positions, then I can sell off a few stock shares to buy the options. However, this has never been an issue for me thus far. You will also see a real-life example of how one might manage a portfolio in the upcoming EBH case study.

Do You Ever Exercise the Options?

When people discover that I buy puts to insure my stock shares, one of the common questions is: *"Do you ever exercise your puts?"* The quick answer is no! This also goes for my call options. Remember, buying a put option gives you the right, but not the obligation to <u>sell</u> 100 shares of stock at a set price on or before a specific date. And if you buy a call option, it gives you the right, but not the obligation to <u>buy</u> 100 shares of stock, at a set price, on or before a specific date.

I'm not telling you never to exercise your options, but I don't because neither of those 'rights' align with my goals. If I want to buy the stock, I buy the stock. I don't need to add the cost of a call option to the transaction. And since I never plan on selling my stock shares, there is no need to exercise my puts, even during a market crash. Some people struggle and almost have a brain explosion when I tell them I don't exercise my puts. They think it's crazy talk. I have these incredible benefits of puts, and I don't use them. They feel it's pointless buying puts if I'm never going to use or exercise them.

But I do benefit from puts. If I ever have a profit on my puts, I book that profit during the annual rebalance of my portfolio. I can then take the profit and use it to buy more options or shares of stock. I also use puts for peace of mind and to help stabilize my account value during severe market crashes. Remember, I want to avoid having my emotions triggered. Ultimately, how put options benefit my account is similar to how bonds work in a portfolio.

Why I Use Put Options Instead of Bonds

Enhanced buy & hold performs and behaves similarly to how stocks and bonds traditionally behave. You may have heard of the 60/40 portfolio. It is comprised of 60% stocks and 40% bonds. The stocks grow your portfolio, and the bonds are designed to provide income, safety, and stability. The 60/40 allocation has withstood the test of time.

However, during the bear market of 2022, it had one of its worst years on record.

In 2022, both stocks and bonds fell in price. This surprised many because, historically, bonds would go up when stocks would go down in price. However, bond price movement is influenced by interest rates, not stocks. When interest rates go up, bond prices fall, and vice versa. Again, bonds fluctuate based on interest rates. They were not designed to make money when a stock falls in price, but puts were.

Stock prices and put option prices, however, do move in opposite directions. When stocks crash in price and lose money, the put option position will make money. That is why I prefer using puts instead of bonds in my portfolio. The extra work involved with resetting the puts each year is no more than what I would have to do with rebalancing a stock and bond portfolio allocation.

Once a year, I decided how many puts, calls, and stock shares to buy. Then I rebalance to keep my allocations where I want them. It only takes me a few minutes a year. I can handle that myself without paying a financial advisor thousands of dollars a year to manage my money. Financial experts say we are not smart enough to manage our money, but I beg to differ.

Speaking of experts, they have done a great job of brainwashing the public on how to invest. If you ask most people about investing in the stock market, they will often tell you to invest in stocks, bonds, or both. Stock options are not even on people's radar. Sadly, they miss out on one of the most powerful wealth-building tools. People are also missing out on the balanced risk that stocks plus options can provide.

What About Time Decay on the Options?

A downfall of buying calls and puts is that they only make money if the market trends strongly in either an up or down direction. If the market trades sideways in any given year, the option positions will lose money primarily due to time decay. The closer options get to their expiration day, the greater the effect time decay has on them. Time decay overview: a long time until expiration, time decay will be minimal and will have a small impact. With a short time until expiration, the option's time decay will be significant.

Thus, I buy long-dated or LEAP options because they are the least affected by time decay and give me protection against the market trading sideways in a given year. Even if it does, I reset my options the next year to buy more time. Said another way, I created a system that protects me against time decay. In summary, time decay with this blueprint is a non-issue, so I won't spend any more time discussing it.

Can You Use EBH With Individual Stocks or Other ETFs?

As you discovered in an earlier chapter, I only invest in the S&P 500. I used to invest in individual stocks, bonds, international stocks, mutual funds, and a whole list of other things. But as I stated earlier, just buying the S&P 500 has been, by far, the most straightforward strategy for me. However, people often ask me if enhanced buy & hold can be used on individual stocks.

Individual stocks are far too volatile; it's not uncommon for a stock to crash in price overnight. Thus, one should always pair up stock purchases with put options. Of course, if the stock rises in price, puts will drag down your overall performance, and that's where call options can help. In up markets, the super performance of calls will help offset the loss on your put options. You'll see an example of this in a later chapter.

So yes, in theory, one could use other ETFs or individual stocks. However, I only have experience with what is shown in this book. The stock would need listed options available to trade, but if I ever decide to invest in individual stocks again, I will use EBH!

Can You Save Money and Only Buy Stock Insurance When You Need It?

Can you predict when you will need put options (aka stock insurance)? I can't, no more than I can predict when

I'll get into a car accident. Thus, I always try to have insurance to protect me from unpredictable tragedies. If I knew when tragedy would strike, I would save money on insurance and would only buy it right before the incident.

Is There an Alternative Way to Grow My Large Account?

This is a variation to the above question. Basically, people try to avoid buying puts because of their cost and how much they hinder their portfolio's performance. I can't tell you what to do, but if I couldn't get over the psychological hurdle of buying puts, here is what I would do. I would follow an 80/10/10 formula.

I would put 80% of my money in SPY stock shares, 10% in call options, and 10% in cash. I would then rebalance at the end of each year as usual. I'd leave 10% in cash because one day, I will lose 100% of my call investment. I would use that cash to start over with my call allocation. Of course, this is all theory because I don't mind buying puts, and I already explained why I use them.

In conclusion, enhanced buy & hold has been my secret to beating the stock market average and protecting our six- and seven-figure investment accounts. But what if you do not have a large investment account? Well, that is what we will cover in the next chapter. You will discover how to grow a small investment account into a large one.

9

HOW TO GROW A SMALL ACCOUNT INTO SIX FIGURES

If you have a dream AND you have a job. That's amazing! You can learn how to navigate both. Your employer, or as I like to call it your 'investor,' gives you the money to invest in your dream, and pay your bills while you chase your dreams.

— LISA NICHOLS

Disclaimer: None of what is presented in this chapter, and the next few, is investment advice. It is all for illustrative, informational, inspirational, and educational purposes only. I am merely sharing what we did to achieve financial freedom. Early retirement is a dream for many, but there are no guarantees with the stock market. All we can do is follow a proven blueprint and hope for the best while being prepared for the worst.

As with all investing, your results will vary based on your capacity, experience, expertise, dedication, and level of desire and motivation. There is no assurance that the examples of successful past performance can be duplicated. You also may be unable to manage the blueprint as flawlessly as in the upcoming case study. As you know, life can be messy and complicated at times. It is rarely perfect. With those lovely statements out of the way, let's get to the good stuff.

As explained, the enhanced buy & hold blueprint is ideally suited for people with six- or seven-figure investment accounts. However, I do not want small account investors to feel left out. I grew up American poor, so I know how it feels to be excluded and forgotten about. Thus, in this chapter, you will discover how one minority, who grew up poor in a house with no running water or bathroom, grew his small trading account and achieved financial freedom at the age of 34. Note: His household toilet was a 5-gallon paint bucket.

And yes, the previous statement may sound a little *'too good to be true.'* Like something you would hear on a late-night infomercial. Honestly, it's my story; I live it, and even I have a hard time believing it. That is why I FULLY expect you to verify every claim I make in this book. It's what any prudent investor would do. So please hold your judgment until you verify everything I am saying.

But yes, I left corporate America when I was 34. And yes, I'm an investor who used stock options to achieve financial freedom with a relatively small trading account (I was told I needed millions). However, there was nothing quick or easy about my journey! Real wealth is built over time, not overnight.

So, if you happen to be one of the many suckers looking for a secret to getting rich quickly with no work on your part, please go elsewhere. You won't be ready to hear my message until you are clean and off that drug. Like anything worthwhile, it will take a lot of effort and persistence before you succeed as a stock market investor. Said another way, there is no overnight fix to poverty. I have not discovered a secret to take you from broke to rich overnight.

I have, however, discovered that the more you sacrifice, the quicker you can build wealth. So, for those who are more mature in their expectations, I will share our approach to growing our $10,000 account into a $100,000 in the stock market. And then, in a few chapters, I will share how we manage this larger portfolio with the enhanced buy & hold blueprint.

I was able to leave corporate America once we hit $100,000 because the portfolio generated $2,000–$5,000 a month in profit. We were debt free, lived in a paid-off

700 sq. ft home, and only had one newborn son. So that was enough for us to live off. Now, three kids later and living in a much bigger house, more than $100K would be required. Regardless, I want to show you how we grew our small trading account into a six-figure account . . .

You start with $10,000, and your goal is to grow your account by 60% for five years. If you do that, you will have $104,858 at the end of five years. My wife and I were fortunate enough to hit that six-figure goal, but in full disclosure, we had a crazy high savings rate.

Here is what the five-year journey looks like:

- Year 01: $10,000 to $16,000
- Year 02: $16,000 to $25,600
- Year 03: $25,600 to $40,960
- Year 04: $40,960 to $65,536
- Year 05: $65,536 to $104,858

So, $100,000 in five years is the goal, but life may work out differently for you. One of the things that helped my wife and I was taking a Financial Peace University class. It showed us a systematic and proven way of paying off our debt. Being debt free allowed us to live off one person's corporate income and save and invest the other person's income. I estimate we had a 60–70% savings rate. And yes, I know that such a high savings rate is unconventional for most of the population, but it is what we did.

Conventional lifestyle choices rarely produce an unconventional life (i.e., financial freedom in your 30s).

The American consumer culture teaches you to spend all your money and enjoy life now. However, you often end up broke in the future. Also, traditional retirement dogma convinces you to live poor and invest in mutual funds to retire rich in your late 60s. Yeah, no thanks to both! We wanted financial freedom while we were still young, not when we were older and when health and energy were fading. Thus, we made extreme short-term sacrifices to save money so that we could live the rest of our lives any way we wanted.

And that leads to one of the most critical aspects of our 5-year retirement plan. We did **not** get 60% growth purely from the stock market! That's impossible for most people. Thus, we got 60% growth through personal savings and investment performance. In the first few years, most of the 60% growth will come from money you deposit into the account.

Now that we have covered the big-picture overview of what it takes to grow a small account quickly, it's time to delve into the 'how to.' We will walk through a 'bonus' case study outlining the step-by-step process of growing a small $10,000 account into a six-figure one. Then in the following chapter, you will discover how to manage the larger account with enhanced buy & hold.

We will cover a lot of math, so I will introduce two fictional characters named Sam and Sara to make the following few chapters easier to digest. They represent the clients I have worked with over the years. However, I changed their names and personal details to protect their privacy.

As already explained, personal contributions are required for the plan to work effectively. After all, you must develop a strong habit of saving money to build wealth. However, like most Americans, Sam and Sara lived paycheck to paycheck and had very little money left over at the end of the month. They were in the habit of experiencing the short-term benefits of consumerism, but the long-term consequence was a lack of personal wealth.

However, they were now committed to achieving financial freedom and made a few *'temporary adjustments.'* They chose a short-term consequence of cutting back on their spending in exchange for the long-term benefit of financial freedom.

- They decided to reduce going out to eat four times a week to one.
- They canceled their cable TV subscription and reduced their cell phone plan.
- And they made a few other minor sacrifices.

In total, they were able to free up $550, which they were now going to have automatically deposited into their trading account each month. In addition to that, they committed to depositing their yearly tax return of $3,200 to the account.

Next, Sam decided to follow an aggressive approach to investing. One of the pros of this approach is that it can grow a small account quickly, but it's riskier. Thus, **it's best not to follow this approach for the long term**.

The aggressive growth plan Sam followed is simply using the two most profitable components of the EBH blueprint:

- Buying the long-term Buffett SPY call option (aka LEAP calls).
- Buying shares of the SPY ETF.

Having only stock shares and calls can allow you to achieve a level of super performance that people assume is unachievable. This setup is similar to the aggressive growth allocation my wife and I used to grow our small investment account. The only difference is that my wife and I used a 20% option allocation (i.e., risked the money on calls), and then we left the rest of our account in cash.

At that point in my investing career, I was not a strong believer in buy & hold. I was still turned off by the slow growth of it, as well as the negative downfalls of having inadequate bear market protection. However, now that I am experienced with buying stock insurance, I have integrated buy & hold back into my investment process.

Regardless, the 80% cash and 20% options allocation still allowed us to grow our accounts fast. The downfall was that I woke up fifteen years later with a high-paying job (active trading). If I did not trade, I did not make any money. If I were starting over today, I would use the above two steps to grow our accounts. This way, we could use our option profits to build up our passive buy & hold income machine.

Now for the warnings. One of the downfalls of the above two-step approach is that it's too risky to use long term or with bigger accounts. The larger your account gets, the bigger the losses and the harder it will be to recover from them. For example, it's easier for most people to recover from a $10,000 loss versus a $100,000 loss.

You may lose 100% of your money on the options one day! That's why we risk so little of our money on options. And it's another reason personal contributions are so vital initially. When, not if, but when you lose a lot of money with this aggressive approach, you can usually add more money to your account and recover quickly.

However, once the account nears $100,000, we shift to a safer and more conservative approach. We add buying put options in the third step of the EBH blueprint. This demonstrates that an intelligent person does not run away from the risk of losing money with options. Instead, they intelligently manage the risk. With that out of the way, let's move on to the next chapter, where we will look at what this 5-year retirement plan would look like using the period from 2010 to 2014.

SAM'S JOURNEY FROM $10,000 TO $93,000

An investment in knowledge pays the best interest.

— BENJAMIN FRANKLIN

Y ou are about to watch Sam grow his small account using the principles covered in the previous chapter. Then in a later chapter, you will discover how they use enhanced buy & hold to grow and protect their wealth.

Although Sam is the one who manages the family's money, his wife Sara is kept in the loop with what is going on. They start this in September because the kids are back in school, and they have the time to focus on other projects. Also, starting later in the year demonstrates the random entry nature of the template. It can be entered at any time, and then at the end of the year or beginning of the following year, you will reset the option positions. Resetting means closing your current options and buying new ones with a new expiration date. Lastly, the prices covered in the case study are historical prices of the SPY ETF and the accompanying call and put options.

Start Date: September 13, 2010 (Starting amount: $10,000)

- SPY is trading @ $112.72

For simplicity reasons, Sam buys a call option with a strike price closest to or at the same price as the stock (the at-the-money option). Since he is not buying puts, he invests 20% of his account into call options.

- Sam buys two December 2012, 115 strike call options for $13.20. A total investment of $2,640. That's slightly over 20% of the total account value.
- With the remaining funds of roughly $7,300, Sam buys 65 shares of SPY.

Again, the 115 strike price is considered the at-the-money option because it is the closest to the stock price. This ATM strike price choice will be repeated throughout the case study because it's an easy rule for beginners to follow.

The total investment between the calls and stock shares is $9,966.80. There is nothing further to do except watch the portfolio to see how it performs monthly. The next time Sam will tinker with his portfolio is during the annual rebalance. Let's fast forward to see what that would look like …

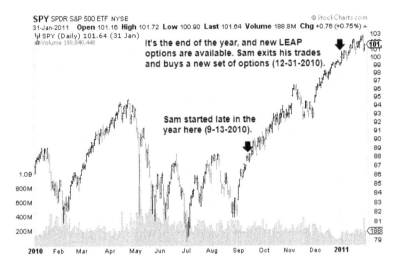

Figure 6 Stock chart of SPY during the year 2010, Source: StockCharts.com

December 31, 2010 (the annual portfolio rebalance)

Last year, Sam started with $10,000; with it, he bought two call options and 65 shares of SPY stock. Let's check in to see how his positions performed:

- SPY stock is trading at $125.75 a share. The 65 stock shares had a profit of **$846.95**, or an 11.6% increase. That is the buy & hold return.
- Sam does not sell his stock shares as the plan is to hold them long term. They are never meant to be sold unless Sam or Sara needs the cash.

Now let's see how the call options performed:

- He sells his two call options for $20.21 a contract.
- He achieved a profit of **$1,402**, or a 53% return on investment.

The options profit was larger and risked less money than buy & hold. This, again, illustrates how options create the 'enhanced' part of this buy & hold blueprint. If we divide the combined stock and options profit of $2,248.95 by Sam's starting balance of $10,000, we get a total account growth of 22.49%. It's almost double the buy & hold return of 11.6%. I'd say Sam achieved a 'market-beating' return. And when you discover a way to achieve double what buy & hold generates, you have found a way to build wealth rapidly. But again, don't forget that losses are also a part of all successful investing.

———

Speaking of losses, let's pause here to talk about losing money (yet again). Yes, the call option return of 53% was incredible, but don't get so excited that you forget the leverage also works in reverse. **It's best never to forget that.** How would you feel if you had lost 53% of your investment? You will see a loss like that later in the case study.

Too many people use options to get rich fast and often go broke. That's why there are more crash-and-burn stories than rags to riches. So please understand that I'm not trying to act like your parent, but I am one of the few who have survived the options game for over twenty years. Many have failed, primarily because they didn't focus enough on protecting themselves from losing money. Okay, back to the case study . . .

It's the end of the year, and the new December option expirations are listed, so it's time for the annual reset/re-balance of the option positions. Again, the yearly reset means closing your current options and buying new ones with a new expiration date. Since Sam started late in the year, he could not add many personal contributions. Their tax refund was spent months ago, and he, and his wife Sara, only had $2,500 in automated savings deposited to the account. At this point, Sam runs the calculations to figure out how much to devote to call options.

Moving forward, this calculation will be run behind the scenes to figure out Sam's account balance. We will add the following figures together: (# of SPY stock shares owned * the current price of SPY) + the cash generated from selling the option positions + the personal contributions = the current account balance. Here are Sam's calculations:

- 65 shares of SPY * $125.75 = $8,173.75
- + $4,042 cash from selling last year's two call options
- + $2,500 in personal contributions
- = a new account balance of $14,716

And the account balance multiplied by 0.2 = $2,943. That amount is 20% of his account value and roughly what he invested in the next round of call options. Remember that Sam never sold his stock shares, so his only available cash is $6,542. It's the money he deposited into his account and the cash he received from selling his old call options.

- With this cash, he buys two December 2013, 130 strike call options for $14.50 a contract. A total investment of $2,900 for both call options.
- With the remaining cash, he buys another 26 shares of SPY. He now owns 91 shares in total.

Sam now owns 91 shares of SPY, two call options, and an insignificant amount of the account is sitting in cash, uninvested. Moving forward, to keep the math in the case study simple, I will ignore the uninvested cash and their stock dividend payments. Also, since Sam will be in these option trades for at least a year, we will consider this the start of year one. Now we fast forward to next year . . .

Figure 7 Stock chart of SPY during the year 2011, Source: StockCharts.com

January 03, 2012 (The end of year one and the time to reset/rebalance the options)

From this point on, I will only reference the price and profit of SPY for comparison. We are mainly focused on managing the option positions on a year-to-year basis.

- SPY is trading at the price of $127.50 a share. A 1.4% increase since last year.
- Sam doesn't sell his 91 stock shares as the plan is to hold these for the long term. But he does sell his two call options for $14.06 a contract. He took a **slight loss of $88, or -3%.**
- Also, his twelve $550 deposits, plus his tax return, equaled $9,800 in personal contributions.

He then performs the rebalance, i.e., he takes his available cash and buys new call options and stock shares. He takes his account balance of $24,215 and multiplies it by 0.2. He will invest roughly $4,843 in the next round of at-the-money call options.

- Sam buys three December 2014, 130 call options for $17.91 a contract. A total investment of $5,373, a little more than 20% of his account balance.
- With his leftover cash, he buys 56 more shares of SPY. He now owns 147 shares in total.

Sam is a bit bummed about his call option loss, so he has me look at his portfolio to see if he did anything wrong. Here is a snippet of our conversation:

"Hey, Sam, before we begin, I want to ask, did you contribute to your account this year?" Sam sarcastically responds, "Yes, that's the only reason our account is higher."

"Sam, your sarcasm has been noted, and I truly understand how you feel. First, I want to congratulate you on committing to adding money to the account. When you are growing an account, that's the most crucial piece. However, do not make the same mistake many others make. The mistake of only focusing on your stock market performance. This causes your brain to miss an obvious truth staring you in the face. Let me point it out to you.

Sam, you started with $10,000 and now have roughly $24,000.

"You have more than doubled your account in a little over a year! If you keep pressing forward, millionaire status could be yours. Remember, this is the exact blueprint my millionaire mentor shared with me. It worked for me, and now it's working for you. However, some people do not like this approach. Sadly, I once had a guy get crabby with me when I showed him this plan. He said adding money to the account was cheating, and he wanted me to show him how to grow his account by 60% purely from trading profits. I have been investing for nearly two decades and have yet to find anyone who can consistently do that."

"Thanks, Travis. I hear you, but watching my account wiggle around all year and ending with a call option loss was disappointing. Especially knowing that I had a $600 call profit earlier in the year. Is there anything I can do about that? Why don't we capture the profit while we have it before the market takes it away?"

"Yes, you can use a short-term trading template to capture the short-term profits, but it's more time-consuming, and you must constantly watch the market. Short-term templates can be mentally exhausting. Lastly, you are assuming you will have the time to constantly watch the market and capture profit at the perfect time. It rarely works out that way. Life will constantly get in the way.

"At least with the Buffet call option you are using, you can place the trade and ignore the market for an entire year. Remember, we are modeling the success of Warren Buffett. We do not concern ourselves with the short-term movement of the market. We are looking to take advantage of the long-term trend of American capitalism. That said, your feelings are normal. Newer traders struggle with this template because it forces you to strengthen the two ingredients necessary for investing success, discipline and patience. You cannot succeed without those two qualities, so you set yourself up for future success by mastering this template now.

"With those rambles aside, we do have a way to capture the profit of the options before the market takes it away. It's during the annual rebalance. When we close the option trades each year, we . . .

1. Capture any profit we have.
2. Take advantage of the newly listed LEAP options. And . . .
3. We get a lower tax rate since we held the trade for over a year. Of course, inside of a retirement account, there are no tax considerations."

Sam responds, "Okay, I get that. I've already rebalanced everything, but is that it? Am I done? It only took me about 15 minutes to set everything up. I feel like I am missing something or that there is something else I should be doing."

I smile because I can relate, then respond, "You know, I've had a few clients mention the same thing. Those of us who grew up in working-class households were programmed with the belief that you must work hard for money. So when we use a passive investing system, it takes some getting used to. But yes, you are done for the year. Watch your portfolio over the next few months to learn how the stock's movement affects the call options in up and down markets.

"Lastly, it's your money, and I can't give financial advice, but I suggest leaving your portfolio alone, no matter how the stock market performs. You will be tempted to tinker with it if you either make a lot of money or lose a great deal. Resist the temptation. You have to give the system a fair chance of proving its validity. It's the long-term results we are after, not the short-term ones. Again, we are trying to have a long-term mindset like Buffett."

"Okay, Travis, I'll try to keep that in mind, but I can't make any promises."

January 04, 2013 (The end of year two and time to rebalance the portfolio)

- SPY is trading at the price of $146.37 a share. A 14.8% increase from the previous year.
- His three calls achieved a gain of $1,503, or a 28% return on his investment.
- And once again, his contributions were $9,800.

Sam runs the yearly calculations to see how much he will invest in the next round of call options. He takes his account balance of $38,192 and multiplies it by 0.2. He will invest roughly $7,638 in the next round of at-the-money call options.

- Sam buys six December 2015, 150 call options for $14.76 per contract. A total investment of $8,856 is 23% of his account value.
- With his leftover cash, he buys 53 more shares of SPY. He now owns 200 shares in total.

Since Sam is busy with life, we do not meet this year, but he does send me an email update. He states that he is much happier with his performance this year and cannot believe he did so well, even though he hardly looked at his account all year. He had a tough year personally, so the passive system was perfect. All you need to do is sell your option positions, calculate 20% of your new account value, and buy a new set of options. And if you have any leftover cash, you can buy more stock shares. This is doable if a person has 10 to 15 minutes once a year. Now that you are familiar with the routine, I will summarize the next few years of performance.

January 06, 2014 (The end of year three and time to rebalance the portfolio)

- SPY is trading at the price of $182.36 a share. A 24.6% increase from the previous year.
- His six calls achieved a gain of $13,122, or a 148% return on his investment.
- This year, they have personal contributions of $11,000 versus the $9,800 from previous years. They paid off one of their credit cards and added the previous payment of $100 to their trading account.

Sam's new account balance is $68,250, and 20% of that amount is $13,650. He buys eight at-the-money call options and 91 more shares of stock. Their account now consists of 291 shares of SPY stock, eight call options, and an insignificant amount of uninvested cash.

During our annual meeting, Sam tells me his wife Sara is skeptical because the results seem too good to be true. She wanted to know if he was doing anything illegal. I've heard that before, and I do understand. These results seem too good to be true, which is why so few people believe me when I tell them I can consistently beat the market's performance. Also, since Sam's account is growing, and his call profits are much larger, I share some wisdom with him.

"Sam, now that you see the power of call options, you may be tempted to risk more money on them. If so, the temptation is normal because most people are not accustomed to earning such high returns on their money. It takes a while to master how it negatively influences your emotions. So monitor your emotions, and if your emotions get triggered too much (greed or fear), you need to scale back on your risk."

Sam replies, "Thanks for the tips, Travis. I will keep that in mind. See you next year."

January 07, 2015 (The end of year four and the end of the small account case study)

- SPY is trading at the price of $202.31 a share. A 10.9% increase from the previous year.
- His eight calls achieved a gain of $8,528, or a 56.6% return on his investment.
- They have $11,000 in personal contributions again, and they still own 291 shares of SPY.

Sam and Sara's new account balance is $93,472. Since that is close to $100,000, I told them it's time to introduce them to the enhanced buy & hold blueprint.

"Well, Sam, I have good news and not-so-good news. The good news is that it has only been four years, and you have grown a $10,000 investment account into $93,472. You have achieved remarkable growth if you ask me. The not-so-good news is that since you are close enough to a six-figure investment account, it's time to implement the full enhanced buy & hold blueprint."

Sam replies, "I think that's exciting, but why do you say it's not good news?"

"Great question, Sam. The summary is that the market crash protection component of EBH will hinder the port-folio's growth. You will no longer experience fast growth. However, it still should be possible to beat the perfor-mance of the S&P 500 over the long term. Of course, I cannot guarantee that, but that is what I and other clients have been able to do. Also, after seeing how fast call options grow your account and how much put options slow it down, you will be tempted to get rid of the puts and continue the aggressive call/stock position. Please don't do it! It would be a mistake. That bad habit will catch up with you at the worst time, and you will lose a lot of money. I'm telling you what I know from my own experience and watching option traders fail over the years."

Parting Thoughts Before We Move On

The story you just read was a big-picture overview of what my wife and I did to grow our investment account fast. We combined high savings with a prudently aggressive approach to trading options. I also want to make sure I stress the fact that these results are not typical. Typically, people don't grow $10,000 into $93,000 in four years, but it is possible for those willing to commit to the plan and have the discipline to save money.

Lastly, were you inspired by what is possible when you combine stocks with options? Are you excited about the possibility that in just a few short years, you could have a much bigger account? If so, sign up for a FREE video demonstration of the Buffett call at: www.tradertravis.com/bookbonus.html.

11

THE EBH CASE STUDY: $93K TO $194K

The stock market goes up or down, and you can't adjust your portfolio based on the whims of the market, so you have to have a strategy in a position and stay true to that strategy and not pay attention to noise that could surround any particular investment.

— JOHN PAULSON

This chapter will continue Sam and Sara's case study, but primarily as casual observers. Sam and I will not have much dialogue, but I will add commentary to highlight important lessons.

You witnessed Sam becoming richer faster by investing aggressively with a little bit of money (less than $100K). But to stay rich, Sam needs to shift gears and invest conservatively. He is experienced with two of the enhanced buy & hold steps, buying LEAP calls and SPY shares. Now, you will watch Sam add in the third and final step, buying LEAP put options for market crash protection.

January 07, 2015 (The beginning of the EBH case study)

- SPY is trading at the price of $202.31 a share. A 10.9% increase from the previous year.
- Sam sells his eight December 2016, 185 strike call options for $29.50 a contract. He achieved a gain of $8,528, or a 56.6% return on his investment.
- They have $11,000 in personal contributions again, and they still own 291 shares of SPY.

Sam and Sara's new account balance is $93,472. Since that's close to $100,000, they shift to the enhanced buy & hold blueprint. With EBH, Sam no longer has to calculate 20% of his account value. The option rules are now more simplified. How many option contracts he buys is based on the number of stock shares he owns.

They have $34,600 in cash from personal contributions, as well as selling their old call options. Sam already owns 291 shares and is getting close to the transition point of 350 shares. Thus, he buys four calls, and four puts, so they are already in place once he obtains more shares.

- Sam buys four December 2017, 205 strike calls for $24 a contract and four 205 puts for $30.59. A total cost of $21,836 for the calls and puts.
- With the leftover cash, he buys 63 more shares of SPY. He now owns 354 shares in total.

Sam asks, "What about our contributions? Do we still add those to the account?"

"Great question, Sam. Yes, you can. Usually, with this blueprint, I work with retirees who are no longer contributing to their accounts. Their focus is mostly on growing their retirement accounts without losing it all. But you can use that to your advantage since you are still working. The more cash you contribute to this money machine, the faster you can retire."

Sam then tells me they paid off one of their cars, and since it's still reasonably new, they decided not to get a new one. They will add the freed-up $450 to the trading account. From this point on, their yearly personal contributions will be $16,400.

Sam then reveals an insight I have heard from others who have made similar sacrifices. "Travis, it's funny; we never realized we had so much disposable income because it all went to debt payments. However, once we automated our savings, we found it easier to live on less."

"Yes, Sam, that is usually how it works, but most people never discover that because they do not even try. They have their minds made up that it would be impossible to cut back on expenses, but a person will never know unless they try. So congrats to you and your wife. I am proud to be a small part of your financial freedom journey. I'll see you at next year's check-in."

January 08, 2016 (The end of year one of EBH and time to rebalance the portfolio)

- SPY is trading at the price of $191.92 a share. A 5% decrease from the previous year.
- Sam sells his four calls for a loss of $4,572, or a -47.6% return on investment.
- He also sells his four puts for a loss of $244, or a -2% return on investment.
- The combined loss on the calls and puts is $4,816.
- They have $16,400 in personal contributions and still own 354 SPY shares.

"Well, Sam, you lost money in your first year of using enhanced buy & hold. It does not seem so enhanced, does it? Or maybe it does because the percentage loss on the call was so high. At least you got to see what I always mention about the call options. The market only dropped 5%, and you lost 47% of the money invested in those calls. Just imagine how much you would lose if the market fell further. As you can see, you can both make and lose large sums of money with options. Most people are so enticed by the big gains that they forget about the losing money part. This, again, is why we invest so little of our money into options."

"Yeah, I hear you, Travis, but our account has grown so much over the years that it's not even a big deal. It is simply the price we pay to get rich in the stock market. But I do see what you mean. We took roughly a 50% loss on our call investment, but since we invested so little of our account, it did not destroy our account value. We basically just gave back last year's profit."

"Exactly, Sam! Now you are beginning to think like a prudent investor. The greedy investors are so influenced by the gains that they invest more money. Then when they take a loss, they give back all their gains and some! Yeah, no thanks. I've been there and done that and would rather not revisit that horror story."

Sam chimes in, "You and I both! One last thing before I forget. We both received cost of living raises at work so we could contribute more money to the account. However, we have been thinking about what you said about getting out of all consumer debt. The trading account is doing well, so any extra money we free up will be used to pay off our remaining debt. The quicker we are debt free, the quicker we can consider retiring early."

Unbeknownst to us, while Sam and I were talking, Sara ran the rebalance calculations to make sure she understood everything. She was correct on the math, so . . .

- Sam buys four December 2018, 195 strike calls for $22.26 a contract and four 195 puts for $30.29. So it costs $21,020 for the calls and puts.
- With his leftover cash, he buys 64 more shares of SPY. They now own 418 shares in total.

I will share the math Sara performed now, but moving forward, it will be calculated behind the scenes.

How to Calculate Their Account Balance

- 354 shares * 191.92 stock price = $67,940.
- $17,020 cash from selling last year's four calls and puts.
- $16,400 in personal contributions.

If you add all three figures, you get their new account balance of $101,360. Then the last two figures are added together, $33,420. This will be the cash they have to buy new options and stock shares.

Before we move on to their next year's check-in, I want to comment on their results. This was their first year of using enhanced buy & hold, and they experienced a loss. This, for sure, would be a disappointment to any investor who thought EBH was a magic push-button solution to instant riches. I doubt Sam feels this way because naive investors like that rarely, if ever, grow their accounts to the six-figure size as Sam did. They, instead, get impatient with the slow grind of building wealth and then go off to chase bright shiny objects that promise them a fast and easy path to wealth.

I am speaking from experience. I tried to get rich quickly with little to no work and failed. My desire to get rich in six months kept me from getting rich in six years. My account grew once I matured, subdued my desires, and focused on small, consistent gains. You just witnessed the same thing with Sam's account. He grew a small $10,000 account to six figures in roughly five years. I doubt that would have happened if Sam tried to double his account every year. At least, it never did for me.

Moving on . . .

January 09, 2017 (The end of year two of EBH and time to rebalance the portfolio)

- SPY is trading at the price of $226.46 a share. An 18% increase from the previous year. The 418 shares of stock had an unrealized gain of $14,438.
- Sam sells his four calls for a gain of $7,280, or an 82% return on investment.
- He also sells his four puts for a loss of $7,388, or a -61% return on investment.
- The call and puts balance each other out for a combined loss of $108.

- They have $16,400 in personal contributions and still own 418 SPY shares.

Sam and I meet to review his results for the year as usual. I knew the option performance would be a concern of Sam's, so I pointed out the obvious and tried to focus on the positive.

"Your stock shares had a nice gain, and your account has grown to $131,972. Outstanding! However, I see the put and call positions balanced each other out, so you broke even on those. That sucks, but at least you got the gain of buy & hold without the risk of losing a massive amount of money during a market crash. Of course, it would have been great to make money on the options, but at the beginning of this journey, I explained that your growth would slow because of the puts."

Sam shakes his head in agreement but still expresses frustration with the puts. Thus, I try to get him to see things from another angle.

"Sam, I know you are used to making all that gain on the calls and not sharing it with the put, but peace of mind and market crash protection has a price. You are seeing that now. Another thing to remember is that there are three skill sets to building wealth. If you only focus on making money, you may become frustrated.

At this stage in the journey, we are not focused on massive growth only. We are also focused on keeping the money you made so you can grow it over time. Think about it, your 418 shares gained over $14,000, but because of the put, you had no concern about losing money. So the buy & hold shares are protected and can grow over time. Also, since the calls had a gain almost equal to what you lost on the put, your insurance did not cost you anything."

"I hear you, Travis, but it's been two long years, and these puts are killing my performance. I don't know. I'll think about what you said, but I need time to think through this."

I let him know that his frustrations are typical and valid. We then say our goodbyes, and I do not hear from Sam until the following year. I knew he was frustrated, but I had no idea he was frustrated enough to break discipline. He makes a huge mistake, but his inexperience does not realize it is a mistake. He thinks it's an intelligent decision. You can guess what it is. Yup, he did not buy any puts with the next round of trades.

- Out of greed, Sam buys seven December 2019, 230 strike calls for $23.83 a contract. It costs $16,681 for the calls. **He does not buy any puts!**
- With his leftover cash, he buys 91 more shares of SPY. He now owns 509 shares in total.

January 10, 2018 (The end of year three of EBH and time to rebalance the portfolio)

- SPY is trading at the price of $274.12 a share. A 21% increase from the previous year. The 509 shares of stock had an unrealized gain of $24,259.
- Sam sells his seven calls for a gain of $21,917, or a 131.4% return on investment.
- They have $16,400 in personal contributions and own 509 SPY shares.

When we meet, I discover Sam did not buy any puts, and I can tell he is rather pleased with himself. He thinks he has outsmarted the market. I, on the other hand, am disappointed. Regardless, I first congratulate Sam for staying disciplined for nearly seven years. That took a lot of courage and faith, but it has paid off. **He now has an account balance of $194,525.** I then warned him about his mistake. Sam promised not to make that mistake again and immediately put his portfolio back in balance.

- He buys seven December 2020, 275 strike calls for $31.16 a contract and seven 275 strike puts for $27.93. So it costs $41,363 for the calls and puts.
- With his leftover cash, he buys 49 more shares of SPY. He now owns 558 shares of SPY. He owns more options than he needs but will stay with seven contracts until he accumulates more SPY shares.

Despite Sam's recent decision to gamble and get rid of the put options, he has demonstrated remarkable discipline and patience throughout the years. He, like most, discovered that the hardest part of the investing journey is managing your emotions and staying disciplined. Knowing what to do, and getting yourself to do it, are two separate achievements. That is an important distinction that many miss.

To illustrate that point, let me compare it to my weight loss journey. I realized just how hard it was. I first had to educate myself on why I was getting so fat. Done! Then, I had to eat right and work out consistently. Well . . . let's say I'm a work in process in that area, ha-ha.

Regardless, it is a two-step process; learn and then do. The doing has to be repeated until the goal is achieved. Stated another way, I cannot work out or eat great occasionally. I must continue eating right and working out consistently over a long period of time. In summary, **I have to make good decisions, not just one time, but repeatedly until I achieve my desired results.** It's the same with building wealth.

- Step 1: Learn how to get rich.
- Step 2: Run a marathon of discipline, patience, and prudent financial decisions.

Sadly, only a tiny percentage of the population has the stamina to finish the race. But this is what you have witnessed with Sam and Sara's journey. They stayed on track consistently over the years. They have been running an eight-year money marathon. Are you willing to do the same? Are you willing to commit to the process until you achieve financial freedom?

That said, here is how I feel about Sam's decision not to buy put options. He went without put option insurance in one of the high-earning years. His thought process was normal; I have witnessed many do the same thing. The decision to ditch the puts is mainly based on greed and backed up with logic.

Logically it makes zero sense to own put options. They are guaranteed money losers over time. However, not buying the puts was an error in judgment. And that error in judgment, repeated over time, will eventually cause you to lose money. Sam simply got lucky that that market did not crash in the year he made this mistake.

So here is a reminder of why we own the puts and what will eventually happen if you decide to get rid of them. Remember, put options help you with the second two skill sets of wealth building, keeping the money you make, and growing the money you keep. Getting rid of puts is done by people who only focus on making money, which is why they eventually lose a great deal of money. Greed tends to blind you to risk.

Put options also provide peace of mind and protect you from a catastrophic loss of money. Small losses we can deal with and quickly recover from. It's the catastrophic losses we want to avoid. I'll reference the bear market of 2007–2009 to illustrate this point. Sam has been growing his account for nearly eight years, but if he had a stock + call option portfolio during the 2007–2009 bear market, his $131K account would have dwindled to roughly $52K. Fifty-two thousand is close to his balance in year three of his journey.

So one error in judgment, made at the wrong time, could have erased five years' worth of gains.

Also, we cannot predict the future, so who knows if the market performance will be the same moving forward. For example's sake, let's pretend it will be. That means it could take another five years to grow the $52K back to $131K. He would have lost five years' worth of gain and then taken another five years to recoup it. **One mistake based on greed could have set Sam back 10 years financially!** Again, Sam did not outsmart the market. He got lucky that he made his bad decision in an up year.

———

Let me be clear; we do not buy puts because we need them yearly. Buy & hold works fine all by itself, but again, the 50% losses tend to trigger people's emotions too much and cause them to make bad financial decisions. Do you remember Betty's horror story? I have coached through various market conditions and, to date, I have never seen a client panic sell during a market decline if they owned puts. The bear market of 2020 was one in particular. It fell nearly 34% in about a month. It freaked people out, and many sold their stocks out of fear.

Eighty to ninety percent of the time, we do not need market crash protection. However, we buy puts for the same reason we buy house or car insurance. We buy insurance because it protects us against catastrophic losses, and we never know when the unpredictable will happen. We also buy put options because they balance out the volatile nature of call options. You have seen how calls perform in down markets; they lose a lot of money.

So yes, as Sam discovered, put options drag down your overall performance, but it's simply the price we pay to have market crash protection. It's a fair tradeoff. We give up a few gains on the upside to have market crash insurance that most investors do not have. Losing too much money puts people out of business, so the focus should always be on preventing that. You should always think of risk first and profits second. That is how you win the game of investing. Avoid the activities that will cause you to go broke. If you do that, you will find that making money becomes easier.

In conclusion, put options ultimately are protection against ourselves. They protect us from making emotional decisions and panic selling when stocks fall 20–50%. And if you hold and do not panic sell, you will make far more money in up markets than you lose in down markets.

See you in the next chapter, where we will wrap up this case study.

12

THE EBH CASE STUDY: $194K TO $434K

The average man tends to be much more reactive if you look at the purchases and sales that they make...They tend to buy high and sell low, and so an average man should not be playing this game in that way . . .

— RAY DALIO

As you can see, enhanced buy & hold is a relatively simple concept. Each year a portfolio rebalance is performed where you sell the old options and buy a new set of options with a later expiration. If any money is left over, more stock shares are accumulated. Then once you hit the stock share transition point, you increase the number of option contracts.

Also, in case you did not notice, if Sam estimates he will hit the 50-share transition point soon, he may up his number of contracts ahead of time, so they are in place once he hits the transition point. For example, if he owned 600 shares, he may up his number of option contracts to seven calls and puts ahead of time. This way, the options are already in place once he hits the 650-share transition point.

If there is ever a time when they do not have enough cash to buy the needed option positions, they can sell off a few stock shares to buy the options. This was never an issue for Sam and Sara because they were still adding money to their account. But if they ever stop adding money to the account, this could be an issue in the future.

Again, EBH is a simple process but not necessarily easy. As Sam discovered, the hardest part of the investing journey is managing your emotions and staying disciplined for an extended period of time. To my delight, and for his benefit, Sam stays on track and does not repeat the same mistake of not buying puts. When we last left Sam and Sara, it was January 10, 2018, and they had an account balance of $194,525. Now we move on to their next rebalance date.

<u>Please note</u>: Since you understand how to manage the portfolio, moving forward, the stock and option calculations will be run behind the scenes, and Sam's account growth will be summarized.

January 11, 2019: SPY is trading at $258.98 a share. A 5.5% <u>decrease</u> from the last rebalance point.

- Sam's calls lost $8,771, or -40.2%. His puts gained $2,296, or an 11.7% return on investment (ROI).

Their account grew to $195,799, mostly from put option profit and personal contributions. After the rebalance, they own seven calls, puts, and 592 SPY shares.

January 13, 2020: SPY is trading at $327.95 a share, a 26.6% increase since Sam's last portfolio rebalancing.

- Sam sells his seven calls for a gain of $31,500 (or a 142% ROI). His puts lose $13,454 (or a -66.3% ROI).

Their account grew to $296,619. After the rebalance, they own eight calls, puts, and 652 SPY shares. Sam got greedy with the option positions, but it wasn't too reckless. Also, something to note, since they are trying to benefit from the long-term capital gains tax rate, each annual rebalance moves them further into January. This is a non-issue, but if they ever wanted to move the rebalance date back to December or early January, they could wait for a break-even year and then make the necessary moves.

January 14, 2021: Despite the shortest bear market in history, SPY still rose in price to $378.46, or 15.4%, since January 13th of last year. Of course, Sam had complete peace of mind during the market crash because his account was insured with put options.

- Sam sells his eight calls for a gain of $29,672 (or a 106% ROI). His eight puts lost $4,808 (or a -16.5% ROI).

Sam's account has grown to $345,204. After the rebalance, they own eight calls, puts, and 683 SPY shares.

January 18, 2022: The stock market relentlessly moves higher, and SPY rises to $456.49 a share, or a 20.6% increase since the last portfolio rebalance.

- His eight calls gained $44,416 (or a 113.8% ROI), and his puts lost $24,936 (-52.5% ROI).

Sam is ecstatic because his account has grown to $434,159. After the rebalance, they own eight calls, puts, and 723 SPY shares.

Let's pause here to check in on Sam and Sara. In roughly 11 years, they have grown a $10,000 account into nearly half a million dollars. As you can see, enhanced buy & hold can be powerful when combined with an individual's discipline and commitment. They feel rich, and they should. That is a lot of money. Like most in their situation, they are on an emotional high. And that is a dangerous time to make decisions, like their decision to retire Sara (more on this in a bit).

I want to take a moment to reminisce because Sam and Sara's decision for one of them to quit their job resembled the same decision my wife and I made when we were in a similar situation. We were fortunate to enroll in our church's Financial Peace University class. At the time, it was taught by a guy named Dave Ramsey. Mr. Ramsey has been controversial lately with his strong opinions, but I want to give credit where credit is due. His get-out-of-debt plan worked as advertised. That is more than I can say for some crappy trading courses I have purchased.

Dave said it takes most people about two years to get out of consumer debt following his debt snowball plan. Confession: **I did not believe him!** I looked at our meager income and the hundreds of thousands of dollars of debt my wife and I had, and it did not mathematically seem possible.

However, I swallowed my pride, humbly submitted to his teachings, and followed the plan exactly as he taught it. Two years later, we were completely out of consumer debt. We were so pumped that we kept going and paid off the mortgage. It took an additional three years to pay off the mortgage—so five years in total to be completely debt free. We were out of bondage, and it felt good! It is a feeling that words cannot describe. To top it off, our investment account was producing enough income to live off. But enough about me, let's get back to Sam and Sara ...

Sam asks about retiring his wife Sara, and I share my thoughts based on my experiences. Since they easily survived the sharp market decline of 2020, they developed a false sense of confidence that prices would continue upward. Thus, I warned them about making decisions based on an inflated market that has gone straight up in price for the last 10+ years. I also explained that deciding to live off your portfolio should be based on worst-case scenarios rather than best-case scenarios. You cannot expect the stock market to go up every year; that is unrealistic. You should factor in down periods and plan for periods of 1–3 years where your portfolio barely earns any money.

Despite my caution, they decided to move forward with their plan to retire Sara. She wanted to spend more time with the kids before they headed off to college. I can understand their position because, thankfully, they were now debt free. It is now the year 2022, but I want to circle back to January 08, 2016, when Sam told me the following:

"We both received a cost of living raise at work so we could contribute more money to the account. However, we have been thinking about what you said about getting out of all consumer debt. The trading account is doing well, so any extra money we free up will be used to pay off our remaining debt. The quicker we are debt free, the quicker we can consider retiring early."

It has been six years since Sam and I had that conversation, and during that time, they were getting out of all debt, including their mortgage. For the last few years, they have lived solely off Sam's income, including the contributions made to their investment account. Sara's paycheck was mainly used to pay off their debt. They have even saved up a twelve-month emergency fund.

Now that their debt has been eliminated, they want to do a test run of Sara retiring early. Sam will continue working until they have a million-dollar account, and the kids graduate from high school. Then he and Sara plan on cruising around the world while the kids are in college. If the early retirement experiment does not work, and they run into trouble financially, they will live off their emergency fund while Sara looks for another job.

EARLY RETIREMENT FOR SARA

After planning for the worst and hoping for the best, Sara takes the leap. She leaves her corporate job in January of 2022 to spend more time with their two kids before they leave home for college in a few years.

Sam and Sara currently own 723 shares of SPY. Of course, the yearly dividends of roughly $4,200 do not replace Sara's corporate income, but it does not have to. Remember, Sara's early retirement was primarily made possible because they have no debt, and Sam earns enough to support the family. They also have a year's worth of savings to draw from if Sam loses his job. Over the years, they have also been furthering their options education. More specifically, they have been studying ways to bring in additional income through 'option selling.'

There are two general ways to profit with options. As we have covered in this book, you can buy options for accelerated growth. You can also sell options for a consistent income each month. With options selling, you become the person selling the contracts to the option buyers. Selling options are beyond the scope of this book, but I will introduce the strategies here for you to research further.

The beauty of the EBH setup is that it allows you to sell options against your positions safely. Thus, Sam and Sara used a strategy known as out-of-the-money covered calls. Instead of buying calls, you sell them. It is like renting out your stock shares, in the same way people rent out homes. You are temporarily "renting" control of your shares to the option buyer. In summary, you give the buyer of the call the right to buy your stock shares, and for taking on this obligation, you receive money (i.e., the option premium).

In addition to selling covered calls, they sold out-of-the-money put options against their stock insurance. This is known as calendar spreads. It's selling lower-risk insurance policies to other investors. They used these two strategies as a backup to bring in additional income.

Combined, they brought in an additional $22,117 in instant income that they withdrew from their account to put into savings.

Again, it was January 2022 when they made all these moves. They did not know it then, but their excitement and the EBH blueprint were about to be severely tested. If you were paying attention to the stock market in 2022, you know what happened. We entered a bear market, the first year of Sara's retirement. A market crash in the first year of retirement is nearly every retiree's worst fear. Let's see how they did.

January 19, 2023 (The end of year eight of EBH and time to wrap up the case study)

- SPY is trading at the price of $388.64 a share. A 14.9% decrease from the previous year. The 723 shares of SPY had an unrealized loss of $49,056.
- Sam sells his eight calls for a loss of $35,600, or a -68% return on investment.
- He also sells his eight puts for a gain of $7,600, or a 14.7% return on investment.
- They have $16,400 in personal contributions.

Their account went from $434,159 to $373,387 for a total loss of $60,772 or -14%. This was the same as the pure buy & hold return. Their loss would have been worse, but their contributions and put option profit helped. The loss also excludes the $22,117 in option selling profit they brought in. That money was withdrawn from the account for safekeeping.

Luckily, the bear market did not destroy them financially. However, it did cause them to be more cautious with their profit projections moving forward, which is always a good thing. They decided to watch the market for the next year, and if it looks like it's not recovering, Sara will get a part-time job until the bear market is over.

Regardless of what happens with the stock market, they are in a great position financially. They have put in the work to build wealth and rejected the consumerism culture that is prevalent in America. They are much closer to the financial freedom finish line than they would have been if they had not used enhanced buy & hold. They also understand that the stock market will not stay down forever, so they are eager to see what the next few years will bring. This concludes Sam and Sara's journey.

The story you just read was loosely based on my experience coaching traders over the last decade. The case study also exemplifies why some succeed and others fail with investing. It's a mixture of mindset/beliefs, unrealistic expectations, and a willingness to do hard things over a long period. Yup, it often has little to do with finding the right strategy.

Regardless, why did I profile such a lengthy case study? Several reasons. If this was a short-term trading template, you could evaluate it over one year. However, this is a long-term template, so you must evaluate the long-term results. It is also best to see how the EBH portfolio performs over different market cycles—up, down, and sideways.

Finally, it's a great way to show proof of concept that these strategies work. Then when you start implementing the blueprint yourself, you will have this book as a reference to always compare to your experience. It will be your guidebook, so you know what to do if you feel lost or nervous.

You will do that, right? Implement? Remember, I shared three ways to verify this blueprint in an earlier chapter. Can I promise that you will achieve the same results if you follow this for 10 years? No! However, if the stock market's performance in the next 10 years is like that of the case study, I do not see why your investment results cannot be similar to what you just witnessed.

FREQUENTLY ASKED QUESTION

After reviewing the case study, you may have the following question: *"The calls lose too much money when the market falls, and the puts constantly lose money. Can we use a market timing indicator and only buy calls and puts when we get a signal?"*

Yes, you can, but I wouldn't recommend it. In my experience, active trading works, but it's certainly more work and not passive. That's why it's important to remember that the blueprint taught in this book is called *enhanced buy & hold*, not enhanced options trading. We intentionally avoid market timing because that's not a successful buy & hold principle.

However, it's a great question and one I once had. I imagined how much better I would do financially if I avoided those massive call option losses and only bought puts during market declines. Then I tested my theories, and I was correct. I did make more money, but I worked harder and sacrificed one of my most valuable assets, time. Deciding to work harder is something I struggled with on the path to becoming wealthy.

After much self-reflection and coaching, I realized my desire to trade the market actively was mainly due to my upbringing. I was raised in a working-class household. In that environment, the more time you work, the more money you make. However, learning from wealthy people taught me the importance of disconnecting time from money. This way, you make money even when you are not physically doing any work. And enhanced buy & hold is a great template if disconnecting time from money is your goal.

———

Lastly, I will finish this chapter with a bonus to assist you on this financial independence journey. Since you purchased this book, you get free access to my real-time case studies. You get to look over my shoulder as I invest my money. This way, you never need to feel like you are in the dark, wondering how the strategy will work in today's market environment. To access those real-time case studies, visit the book bonus page at: www.trader-travis.com/bookbonus.html.

FINAL THOUGHTS

Go confidently in the direction of your dreams.
Live the life you've imagined.

— HENRY DAVID THOREAU

You cannot invest like average people if you want above-average wealth and income. Instead, you must use the tools of the wealthy. However, before reading this book, you may not have known how rich people rapidly built or protected their stock market wealth. Thus, you missed out on riches that could have been yours. You paid the 'ignorance tax,' which is the penalty of not knowing how to do something.

However, that ends right here, right now, today! If you follow the principles in this book, in as little as 10 years, you, too, can potentially be basking in the joy of financial freedom. After all, you know more about options trading and index fund investing than most people in the country.

- How many people do you know who are spending countless hours trying to pick individual stocks when index fund investing has proven to be more straightforward and profitable?
- How many of your peers can successfully buy call options to earn leveraged returns of 50–100% on their money in strong up-trending markets?
- Better yet, how many have a blueprint to insuring their portfolio against market crashes with put options?

You are also informed about the myth that buying options do not work. Yes, if you buy options like a gambling addict trying to get rich, you will most likely lose money.

Fortunately, you discovered a prudent and successful way of buying call and put options. You buy and then hold the option contracts over a long period of time. You follow the same sound principles that make buy & hold successful, which is focusing on the long-term trend of the stock market. You combine the best approaches from the buy & hold world with the safest and most profitable strategies from the options world to create enhanced buy & hold.

More specifically . . .

1. You buy LEAP put options on SPY for peace of mind and market crash protection. This also allows you to make money as stock prices fall, making you less likely to panic sell.
2. You then buy LEAP calls for accelerated growth and possibly pay for the cost of your puts.
3. Lastly, you buy shares of broad-based S&P 500 index fund/ETF for safe and stable returns. It's also for long-term passive wealth building.

However, one downfall of enhanced buy & hold is that it does not grow an account as fast as the LEAP call + stock portfolio. But that is by design. EBH is perfectly balanced and does not tickle your greed gland or trigger your eternal panic button. In summary, EBH helps you avoid making too much money too fast or losing too much money. However, it still puts you in a position to build wealth for the long term.

And although these EBH concepts may be new to you, please know that you are not alone on this journey to financial freedom. Each week I get emails from people like you who take control of their future and diligently work to build financial independence for themselves and their families. Below is a small sample of the notes I receive:

"Doing the Travis 'Insurance Happy Dance.' We just closed our Insurance PUT for an approximate 113% gain. At work yesterday, some of my wife's co-workers asked her how bad we were getting hurt now that we were doing 'options' in the market and if she regretted it. She said, 'No, our mentor has taught us how to insure our trades and protect us, and as a matter of fact, we are making money; how are you doing?' Co-worker: Groan and walk off . . ."

— BRIAN

"I got the best night's sleep that I've had in a long time. I didn't care whether the market went up or down."

— JOHN

"I just want to tell you that I have been nothing but stress free when it comes to the market. I know my risk and have zero worries. This would not have been possible without your knowledge and blueprint."

— MARCI

"What I find interesting is I do not 'hear' your voice. All I hear is the caring, commitment, determination, and genuineness of your teachings to make your students become financially free. So for that, Thank You."

— ELLEN

I am excited for you. Like the clients above, your life is about to change for the better, but only if you act on what is taught in the pages of this book. After all, I did not write this book for you to *know* about this information. I wrote this book so you can *use* this information. Start practicing the suggestions in this book today and remember that building wealth and consistent monthly income takes time, and you will need patience. You will not get rich overnight, but you can get rich over time.

When you take advantage of enhanced buy & hold, you will be on the path to rapidly building wealth, retiring early, and living free from the worry of market crashes. Godspeed and I hope you enjoy the ride on the financial freedom train as much as I do.

One final word from me. If this book has helped you, I would appreciate you leaving a review. Reviews are the best way for independently published books to get noticed and reach more people like you who want to better their financial future. I read every review and welcome praise as well as constructive feedback. Your support makes a real difference and will help improve future books. Lastly, to get your book bonuses, go to: www.tradertravis.com/bookbonus.html.

REFERENCES

Cfa, P. G. (2009, April 3). *Warren Buffett's Comments on Option Investing.* Morningstar, Inc. https://www.morningstar.com/articles/285699/warren-buffetts-comments-on-option-investing.

Coleman, M. (2023, March 20). *SPIVA: 2022 Year-End Active vs. Passive Scorecard.* https://www.ifa.com/articles/despite_brief_re prieve_2018_spiva_report_reveals_active_funds_fail_dent_index ing_lead_-_works/.

Contributor, G. (2019, September 8). A Brief History of Stock Options. *TheStreet.* https://www.thestreet.com/opinion/a-brief-history-of-stock-options-10595277.

Detrixhe, J. (2021, November 22). Options trading is poised to overtake the stock market. *Quartz.* https://qz.com/2092197/options-trad ing-is-poised-to-overtake-the-stock-market.

Light, L. (2022, May 25). How Stock Options Can Help Your Shrinking Nest Egg. *Forbes.* https://www.forbes.com/sites/lawrencelight/2022/05/25/how-stock-options-can-help-your-shrinking-nest-egg/?sh=1287e2f355ea.

Locke, T. (2022, May 10). 3 investing lessons Warren Buffett shared at the 2021 Berkshire Hathaway meeting. *CNBC.com.* https://www.cnbc.com/2021/05/03/investing-lessons-from-warren-buffett-at-berkshire-hathaway-meeting.html (Original work published 2021).

Mohamed, T. (2020, June 12). Mark Cuban compared the day-trading boom to the dot-com bubble. Here's how he saved his $1.4 billion Yahoo windfall from the crash. *Markets Insider.* https://markets.busi nessinsider.com/news/stocks/how-mark-cuban-saved-billions-yahoo-windfall-dot-com-crash-2020-6-1029303375.

Stevens, P. (2021, March 24). This chart shows why investors should never try to time the stock market. *CNBC.* https://www.cnbc.com/2021/03/24/this-chart-shows-why-investors-should-never-try-to-time-the-stock-market.html.

What to Do About This Scary Stock Market. (2016, March 3). Mr. Money Mustache. https://www.mrmoneymustache.com/2016/02/29/what-to-do-about-this-scary-stock-market/comment-page-2.

ABOUT THE AUTHOR

Travis Wilkerson, aka Trader Travis, is a U.S. Army Veteran and 2019 United States Investing Champion (Options Division). For most of Travis's 20-year trading career, he struggled with the following question: How can he, a person who grew up poor, with no Wall Street connections, and only an average I.Q. at best, compete against the best and brightest of Wall Street? The answer is you can't!

Thus, Travis created a simple system for average, ordinary investors like himself. A system that allowed him to win the U.S. Investing Championship while only spending roughly 10 minutes a day managing his options portfolio. He attributes his success to focusing on risk first and profits second. In addition, Travis has mentored thousands of trading students, teaching them the exact strategies he used to go from deep in debt to financially free in only 5 years.

You can connect with me on:

https://www.tradertravis.com

https://twitter.com/tradertravis

Subscribe to my newsletter:

https://www.tradertravis.com/bookbonus.html

Printed in the USA
CPSIA information can be obtained
at www.ICGtesting.com
LVHW022143170324
774744LV00033B/703